Foreword

THE
SMALL
BUSINESS
GROWTH
GUIDEBOOK

Brave Strategies for Authentic Success

LAURA DI FRANCO

Featuring: Karen Hulme Alegi, Sandy Travis Bildahl, Donnie Boivin, Michelle M. Burke, Frank Byrum, Carrie Dahle, S.A. Grant, Meridith Grundei, Melissa Henry, Ann Hession, Holly Jean Jackson, Janine Jennings, Prati Kaufman, DeeAnna Merz Nagel, María del Mar Oliva, Dr. Ahriana Platten, Pauline McGuirk Penedo, Jonathan Probert, Deanna Russo, Susie Schaefer, Kyle Steinle, Tanya Stokes

"*The Complete Small Business Growth Guidebook* is a great read! It's not just another business book, and it's not just another self-development/self-help book. It's the best of both worlds and then some. Each author's story leads to a business growth concept that is real and usable. That is the key to this book's success as a guide for those looking for business strategies from real people who've been there, done that, and lived to tell the tale. To top it all off, there are actionable steps from each author to help you take what you've learned and put it into action. It's a great guide for new businesses and "old" businesses because you never stop learning, growing, and evolving IN business until you exit the business. Bonus: you can even apply many of these concepts to life, too. We all know that life and business go hand in hand so don't hesitate to put these principles and strategies to work in your personal life, too."

Sophie Zollmann, Digital Marketing Expert, Owner & CEO of SophieZo Next Level Business Support

*

"The absolute honesty, bravery, and truth that comes through this book is astonishing. I will need to read it again to get all the profound messages to sink in, but I'm truly proud to be part of Laura's beautiful community. I thank all of them for sharing their stories, and I have learned so much. I'm excited to put some of this into practice in my own business and see where I end up in the next year."

Tara Backes, Projects Made Simple, LLC – Your Small Business Assistant

*

"Two years into running my business and facing burnout, this book could not have come into my life at a better time. It lets me know that, at least mentally, dozens (probably more like hundreds) of other people have been almost exactly where I am right now. All entrepreneurs face burnout at some stage of their business. What makes some walk through those flames of turmoil is whether or not they seek out the help they need. Some of the personal stories in this book really hit home for me, and each one will hit you differently. But the strategies that each author brings to this collaborative guide are both advantageous and inspiring, especially when you read them back to back all in one place. Just think of the thousands of other entrepreneurs living similar experiences all over the country. This book doesn't just show you how hard it can be to own a business.

There are no sob stories here. In fact, each chapter is loaded with not only a gripping personal tale but the lived success of the author. I learned several life-changing lessons about how I should be networking, the methodology for saving and investing the money I have, creating my vision and manifesting my new reality. Reading this book is like hanging out at a summer campfire with the people you aspire to be. I cannot wait to implement the methods I learned here and upgrade my own small business, annihilate my fears, and prevail over my roadblocks until I'm just as prosperous as the authors. Laura's story and the gems of wisdom in this book are resources I will come back to again and again; I feel it in my soul."

Amelia South, Black Sun Farm

*

"This book is an impressive compilation of multiple types of businesses, information, and options that every business owner needs to know. Each chapter highlights struggles and solutions that are top of mind at some point in an entrepreneur's journey. The tools shared and the stories that illustrate them are gold and can serve even the most experienced business owner. We all have moments when the inner voice or the lack of organization gets in the way. *The Complete Small Business Growth Guidebook* covers a wide swath of business types, personal stories, creative solutions, essential how-tos, and tools, as well as steadfast tried and true common-sense actions and solutions. I recommend it for any business owner at any stage. An essential book to own."

Liz Goll Lerner, Enlightened Communication Institute®, Your Inspired Choices® LLC

*

"*The Complete Small Business Growth Guidebook: Brave Strategies for Authentic Success* is the book I've been waiting for! If you're exhausted by left-brain business guides that overload you with strategies but lack heart or right-brain books that inspire your vision but leave you without practical steps, this is your answer. This guide masterfully blends both head and heart, offering actionable tactics alongside soulful insights. Finally, a resource that speaks to both the business and the human behind it."

Ginny Robertson, Founder On Purpose Woman Global Community and Magazine

*

Foreword by Randy Molland

THE COMPLETE SMALL BUSINESS GROWTH GUIDEBOOK

Brave Strategies for Authentic Success

LAURA DI FRANCO

Featuring: Karen Hulme Alegi, Sandy Travis Bildahl, Donnie Boivin, Michelle M. Burke, Frank Byrum, Carrie Dahle, S.A. Grant, Meridith Grundei, Melissa Henry, Ann Hession, Holly Jean Jackson, Janine Jennings, Prati Kaufman, DeeAnna Merz Nagel, María del Mar Oliva, Dr. Ahriana Platten, Pauline McGuirk Penedo, Jonathan Probert, Deanna Russo, Susie Schaefer, Kyle Steinle, Tanya Stokes

The Complete Small Business Growth Guidebook
Brave Strategies for Authentic Success
©Copyright 2024 Laura Di Franco
Published by Brave Healer Productions
Cover design by Tanya Stokes
Interior design and illustration by K.J. Kaschula
All rights reserved. No part of this book may be used or reproduced by any means, graphic, electronic, or mechanical, including photocopying, recording, taping or by any information storage retrieval system without the written permission of the publisher, except in the case of brief quotations embodied in critical articles and reviews.
ISBN: 978-1-961493-46-9
ISBN: eBook: 978-1-961493-47-6

Dedication

To my fellow entrepreneurs, business owners, and business coaches, thank you for generously giving your time, energy, and effort to help build this community and for walking beside me on this path. It takes a warrior. I see you.

Get access to The Brave Healer Resources Vault with master classes, pro-tips, and training for author entrepreneurs here: https:/lauradifranco.com/resources-vault/

Disclaimer

This book is designed to provide competent, reliable, and educational information regarding business growth and other subject matter covered. However, it is sold with the understanding the authors and publisher specifically disclaim all responsibility for any liability, loss, or risk, personal or otherwise, incurred as a consequence, directly or indirectly, of the use and application of any of the contents of this publication.

In order to maintain the anonymity of others, the names and identifying characteristics of some people, places, and organizations described in this book have been changed.

This publication contains content that may be potentially triggering or disturbing. Individuals who are sensitive to certain themes are advised to exercise caution while reading.

The opinions, ideas, and recommendations contained in this publication do not necessarily represent those of the Publisher. The use of any information provided in this book is solely at your own risk.

Know that the experts here have shared their tools, practices, and knowledge with you with a sincere and generous intent to assist you on your business journey. Please contact them with any questions you may have about the techniques or information they provided. They will be happy to assist you further and be an ongoing resource for your success!

Galaxy Girl

Melissa Henry

Galaxy Girl was inspired by the goal of helping small business owners achieve success through mindset, community, and proven strategies. Melissa Henry, Founder of Personal Brandtography™ and Helluva Brand™, used a representative image of the night sky to symbolize that entrepreneurial drive to "shoot for the moon and land amongst the stars." Through collaboration with the lead author, Laura Di Franco, Melissa leveraged her expertise in AI imagery to create the final image that truly captures the essence of expansiveness and the importance of having a supportive community on your entrepreneurial journey. Read more about Melissa in Chapter 4.

Foreword

Randy Molland, CGO, GoBigtoGiveBig

This isn't just another boring business book where the authors give you half a tip to draw you in and then leave you hanging because they didn't want to give away their secret sauce. This is a book of successful business owners who truly want to help you grow your business and are giving you every detail on how to do it.

As a Fractional Chief Giving Officer for many companies and founder of the GoBigtoGiveBig movement, my biggest passion in life is teaching business owners how they can use their businesses to support causes they believe in. Our goal is to help companies make as much revenue as possible, so in return, they can do more good with it. The tips and tricks you will find in this book are going to help you grow your business tremendously, but it's your responsibility to make sure you do good with it.

That is why I'm so proud to call Laura a close friend and client of mine because of how she shows up in this world. She's not afraid to be bold in her pursuit of creating an incredible company because she knows the impact she can make along with it. Laura is not just a business owner, she's someone who truly wants to help make the world a better place and is using her business to do it. From donating a percentage of her book sales, sitting on boards of charities, to volunteering her time, Laura has created a brand that people want to share with the world and attach themselves to.

The authors in this book represent the hard work Laura has put into building a company people are proud to be a part of. When she said she was writing a book and bringing together all of her best connections to share their advice about how to scale and grow a business, I knew it was going to be something special.

I have since had the pleasure of meeting every author in this book and learning about the different skills they're sharing, and I can confirm I was right. This book is something special!

Laura's ability to get her authors to share their skills in a captivating way that draws you in as a reader is some of the best work I've seen. These are not just tips and tricks, these are real-life stories of how these business owners use their skills every day and have created their success by doing it.

I hope you enjoy this book as much as I did and that it helps grow your business to new levels of success because the bigger we go, the more we can give!

Randy Molland, Founder of the GoBigtoGiveBig movement. https://gobigtogivebig.com/

Table of Contents

Introduction | i

Part 1
Business Foundations

Chapter 1
Brave Story Medicine™ | 3
Sharing Words that Build Your Business
Laura Di Franco, MPT, Publisher

Chapter 2
Dream it, Live it | 17
Align Your Mindset for Unstoppable Business Success
Carrie Dahle

Chapter 3
Your Vision Audit | 29
The Missing Link to an Unshakable Foundation for Business Success
Sandy Travis Bildahl

Chapter 4
Express Your Uniqueness | 43
Secrets to a Jaw-Dropping Brand
Melissa Henry

Chapter 5
Soulpreneurs Who Can Sell Are Changing the World | 56
The Soulful Path to Success, Contribution, and Abundance
Ann Hession

Chapter 6
Process Systemization | 68
Business Growth on Cruise Control
Pauline McGuirk Penedo

Chapter 7
Reduce Your Tax Burden | 81
When S Corporation Election is Right for Your Entity
Michelle M. Burke, CPA

Chapter 8
Hyper-Focused Revenue Clarity | 91
Build Your Compass and Business ATM for Consistent Cash Flow
Holly Jean Jackson, CEO, Revenue and Performance Consultant

Chapter 9
Permission Slips from the Universe | 104
Authenticity to Attract the Right Clients
Susie Schaefer, Founder & CEO, Finish the Book Publishing

Chapter 10
Systems Success | 114
Turn Your Job Into a Business that Runs Without You
Jonathan Probert

Part 2
Business Strategies

Chapter 11
Digital Marketing Mastery | 124
The Magic Behind Strategies that Work
Prati Kaufman, Entrepreneur, Marketing, and Human Energy Expert

Chapter 12
Networking That Doesn't Suck | 136
How to Grow Your Influence with Key Partnerships
Donnie Boivin

Chapter 13
Podcasting | 147
The Easy Way to Empowerment, Growth, and Success
S.A. Grant, Founder and Host of Boss Uncaged

Chapter 14
Dare to Be Different | 161
"Your Way" May Be the Best Way!
Dr. Ahriana Platten

Chapter 15
A Business Visual Masterpiece | 172
Graphic Design that Establishes Identity and Sells
Tanya Stokes

Chapter 16
Mastering Instagram | 182
Engagement Strategies that Attract Perfect Clients
María del Mar Oliva

Chapter 17
Leverage Up on LinkedIn | 197
Magnify Visibility and Attract the Right Clients
Deanna Russo

Chapter 18
Demystifying Video for Business Development | 209
Consciously Creating Reality with Your Thoughts
Kyle Steinle

Chapter 19
Speak with SPARK | 222
Strategies to Prepare, Practice, and Present Impactful Presentations
Meridith Grundei, Public Speaking and Presentations Skills Coach

Part 3
Staying Power
(A Smarter Long Game)

Chapter 20
Lifelong Learning | 234
The Key to Business Growth and Evolution
DeeAnna Merz Nagel, D.Th, LMHC

Chapter 21
When Your Business is Stuck | 243
A Results Strategy to Achieve Flow and Success—Again
Frank Byrum

Chapter 22
Protect Your Empire | 259
Legal Documents All Small Business Owners Need
Karen Hulme Alegi, Attorney

Chapter 23
Smart Retirement Planning for Business Owners | 268
The Secrets to Securing Your Future
Janine Jennings

Chapter 24
Discernment | 285
Your Ninja Move for Next-Level Business Decisions
Laura Di Franco, MPT, Publisher

Chapter 25
Success Isn't a Solo Gig| 295
A Community-Building Strategy for Next-Level Growth
Laura Di Franco, MPT, Publisher

Introduction

"Randy, I want to write my first $10,000 check!" Saying that out loud gave me goosebumps.

"I want to make enough money to support the people I love and serve, write bigger checks to the non-profits I love, and have way more fun in life!"

I imagine you, amazing entrepreneur, have similar goals.

By the way, Randy is the phenomenal guy who wrote the foreword in this book. If you skipped that because you're not in the habit of reading forewords, please go back and read. One reason you're holding this book in your hands is that Randy believes in me. We joined forces to go bigger in life and business. I'm immensely grateful to him.

When I dreamed up *The Complete Small Business Growth Guidebook* and this collaboration, I knew we'd change lives—and a lot of them! With the help of this expert cast of successful co-author entrepreneurs, we're about to light the world on fire with generous, purposeful, impactful wisdom and strategy that helps you skip experiments and mistakes, stop guessing, and make a faster impact in the world with your business.

I started my first business, hit my first six-figure year, started another and experienced my first multi-six-figure year, began coaching others, and then helped my son start his first business. I made so many guesses and mistakes and overcame so many failures. It became clear—we need a roadmap for success from people who've "been there done that." We need great coaches and professionals and better advice. And we need experts willing to help the little guys get to the next level. No ordinary roadmap or blueprint to success will do, though, especially at this time and place on the planet when the zombie apocalypse is feeling more like a reality. We need a more practical, conscious, heart-centered, and legacy-driven plan. And I knew it was nothing I'd learn in any traditional business book.

Whether you knew it or not when you signed up, entrepreneurship isn't only a quest for time and money freedom; it's a serious self-development journey. Entrepreneurs are also the trailblazers of a bigger mission to do better for the future of this planet. But without proper guidance, mentorship, and community, it can become a path to self-destruction. This journey is for warriors.

The depressing stats are out there. The article below suggests entrepreneurs are two times more likely than others to have suicidal thoughts: https://www.entrepreneur.com/living/why-entrepreneurs-could-be-at-a-higher-risk-for-suicide/432083

"We aren't meant to do this alone," I almost shouted into the Zoom screen. "Stop trying!"

I remember when I started my first business, I thought doing it alone meant I was being successful. Now I know what else is possible. You can go so much bigger together with a community and people who believe in your vision and want to help you build it.

I've been teaching business strategy (no matter what stage or level of success I achieved) for almost as long as I've been in business (two decades) because I believe:

1. We teach what we most need to learn.
2. You only need to be one step ahead of someone to be able to teach what you know and help them.

3. Paying forward what you learn and giving generously from an open, grateful heart is magical manifesting energy.

From the beginning of my journey, over my 30-year career in holistic healing, and as a successful (two-time) small business owner, I know that people who choose entrepreneurship were born to change the world. Only those warriors have the commitment, drive, and indomitable spirit to succeed when the inevitable challenges come.

While everyone has the potential to be a leader (and we're all learning to be leaders of ourselves), some of us take that responsibility on at another level because we practice connecting to a bigger source that tells us every day: *You got this! You were meant for this!*

The thing is, we actually need so much more than that positive mindset and connection to succeed in the ways we dreamed of when we made the choice to open our business doors.

We start on the path with huge excitement, inspiration, motivation, and energy, but starting, running, and growing a successful small business to the next level requires more than that. That belief in something bigger than you is only one key.

You'll want to quit—a lot. You'll need a community—introvert or not. You'll need ninja moves of mindset—more than you think. You'll need people who've been there and done that and who actually have the time to mentor, guide, and coach you, even after they've "made it." You'll need practical strategies. You'll need to cry some days.

This book is going to give you the tools, strategies, practices, resources, mentors, and coaches for authentic business success. It's a community in a book, ready for you to reach out for more help.

What is authentic success?

It's the kind you achieve on your own terms, being your full-on, badass, unapologetic self, creating your own rules and the business culture and lifestyle that generously feeds and supports you and everyone you love and serve while it changes the world.

You're not doing business as usual—we know that and support it.

Authentic success means you're connected to your purpose, you're giving back to the world, and your vision is so big others want to help you build it. Joy is the byproduct of authentic success, not stress. When stress, overwhelm, worry, and fear become the daily byproduct, pause and take a deep, pelvic bowl breath.

There's a better way.

You define success, and if your bank account doesn't cover the expenses and pay the mortgage, it doesn't matter how successful you feel.

By the way, I know you're not in this to just pay the mortgage. I know you want to live a better life, serve and help people in the world, provide for your family, be able to rest and travel with them, and also give to your favorite world-changing organizations.

The author-experts here not only get it, they live it. Each of them is dedicated to your success because yours is theirs. Your legacy matters to us because your legacy is ours!

Dear small business entrepreneurial badasses, feel the ripple?

My goal is to give you practical strategy, coaching, and a community of heart-centered, purpose-driven, generous, holistic-minded business owners who aren't only successful in business. These people are mastering self-care, thriving mind, body, and soul, and building community. Their businesses are giving back and changing the world. We do this together.

Ready to take it all to another level of awesome?

We're not doing business as usual, and that's what's going to change everything for you!

Not Business As Usual

By Laura Di Franco

An ode to my visionary friends.

We're not doing business as usual
and I want the world to know
how you spend your days
the fire you hold
in your hearts, hands, and souls
the steady gaze you keep on your goals
the glaze of passion you use
as you mold your vision.

Watch as your visionary friends
consistently place and protect
the vision of their legacy in one hand
while skillfully monitoring the pulse of the moment
with the other
awake to every possibility.

Your eyes are always on the prize of gratitude
Your soul always seated
in a powerful speed-dial connection
with the Divine.
You commit, persist, and persevere
wiping the tears
transforming limiting beliefs,
doubt, shame, and fear
into fuel.

The strategy?
To follow the brilliant, undeniable, relentless
ache of your heart
instead of your conditioned mind
to find your true self
in the middle of what you've been told
you should be.

Others sometimes see
and utter, "Fool," under their breath
because they haven't given themselves permission
to lock arms with joy yet
having previously been taught
that the way to success
is the world's way
and not the blissful ecstasy
waiting when you find your own.

Visionaries take chaos, pain, and tragedy
and own every bit
taking full responsibility
for shaping it into brave story medicine
mixing in mistakes and failures
to create a potent brew of inspiration
and freedom.

We're addicts—this recipe for excellence
our drug of choice
every breath an opportunity
for peak performance.
Excuses are not an ingredient.
Neither are blame, comparison, or complaint.
We call bullshit on victimhood.

Visionaries curate their inner circle,
collaborate,
celebrate each other's success
like it's their own.
They host those parties
step up as MC
always showing up as the Jaime Lee
for their friends
because they know what they feel, think,
say, and do
creates a powerful trend
playing out in the now.
That focused energy and intention
is the how.

You may get a call from this wild-ass friend
"Hey, I have this crazy idea," she says.
Heads up.
She's not asking for an opinion.
In her mind the thing's already done
But she knows that
when it's out loud, it's real.
So with you as witness
she's staying accountable to her dreams
and making it happen.
And, a few more things
about these visionary alien souls
We understand our authentic power.
We eat *The Secret* for breakfast.
Our morning, noon, and night are all miracles.
We see the magic in the world
and do business in ways
that've never been done.

Our business is definitely not usual.
Our business is the hero of a soul story
a flame ignited by God
that we feed, nourish, and tend
until the light is bright and hot enough
to reach the stars
bend time.

We climb that ladder of light
every day
to get a rockship's eye view.
We took a deep breath and flew
spreading our wings wide
every time someone said no
not afraid of what we'd encounter on the ride
knowing we're born to fly.

I see you, you badass.
It's time.

Come out and play.
Let's wake them up,
make them pay attention.
Let's change it all.
Let's go.
Cannonball with me
into your discomfort zone.
Let's show them what can be done
when we have fun with the fear
and do the thing
we were put here to do.
It's time.
And I believe in you.

Listen to this poem on the Positively Purposeful Poetry YouTube Channel:
https://www.youtube.com/@positivelypurposefulpoetry8316

Part 1
Business Foundations

There are some business topics I consider foundational—the ones you'll stand on no matter what else you do, build, or try. The chapters in this section cover things like vision, purpose, mindset, branding, selling, systems, and revenue performance. When you set solid foundations, you're unstoppable.

One of the foundations of my business has been storytelling. Some might have put this in the "Strategies" section, but I realized that since the beginning of time, stories are how we connect. Connecting with people is how you make money. Without connection, there is no business. And that's why I asked every author here in this business book to share their real, vulnerable stories.

Chapter 1

Brave Story Medicine™
Sharing Words that Build Your Business

Laura Di Franco, MPT, Publisher

> *Your words change the world when you're brave enough to share them. It's time to be brave. If I could star over, I'd have way more fun with my fear!*

My Story

"They've all heard my story before. I know they must be bored of it by now."

Eight years into my business, I spoke those words to a friend and immediately called myself out on the next-level self-sabotaging bullshit going down.

Oh, crap. Listen to me. This must be that upper limit problem happening again.

Have you read Dr. Gay Hendrick's *The Big Leap*? He taught me about the upper limit problem and helped me with a level of awareness that catapulted my ability to call myself out and pause the habit of paralyzing thoughts that try to drown me when I do big-ass things in the world.

"They aren't bored of it. You've told it so many times that you imagine they are. But they're not, believe me. Every time I hear you tell that story I get goosebumps, and I receive another layer I need to receive."

I appreciate how my friend gently coached me exactly how I coach others. Being coachable is one of my success strategies.

Ha! If only I'd listen to my own advice.

I wasn't tired of telling those stories, and I didn't think they were boring. My problem was the stories I hadn't shared yet—kept-to-myself gems I was afraid others would react negatively to, or worse!

Maybe they won't want to work with me! Gasp!

What will they think?

Oh, how those four little words do their damage.

Wise self: *Who cares what the fuck they think?*

Martha: *Yeah, but...*

Wise self (getting good at interrupting Martha): *No! Stop! You know better. Make that ninja move and flip the switch. It's none of your business what people think.*

Martha: *But...*

Wise self: *Listen, I feel you. I know you're trying to protect me, and I love you for that. But we can do this. It's okay that people don't like you—good even!*

It's okay if they don't want to work with you. You're not for everyone. And you don't want everyone as a client. Be your badass self, girl. That's how you attract the right people.

I love my wise self. She's pretty smart.

I named my inner critic Martha eight years ago when I started my business. Laura Munson taught us how to do that at the Haven Writing Retreat, and it changed my life. Now, instead of instantly being paralyzed by inner critic thoughts, I befriend those parts of me, and we get on with the world-changing badassery together.

I discovered two versions of the inner critic. One came from what people said to me in the past and what I made those things mean. That voice came from putting too much weight on what others think and not trusting my gut or following my joy. I call that voice Martha.

The other voice was my scared little girl. She was silent. There's no voice when she shows up, and that's how I recognize her. She runs away from hard feelings and conflict. She'd rather stay silent and avoid emotions. She's my (recovering) good girl who spent decades making sure you liked her. That voice came from my deep attachment to being loved at all costs and from a black hole of unworthiness that took a lifetime to unwind and heal.

During my thirty years in holistic healing, I practiced integrating all of the parts of me, accepting and loving them. And now, when that little girl shows up afraid, I hold her hand, and we do the scary things together. She's so amazing.

Girl, you're a badass hippie warrior of love; I love you.

ACTION STEP BONUS:

Pause here and create some self-talk that inspires *you*. Go for it. Or feel free to steal mine. Remember to add, "I love you!"

Martha is another story, and she's a bitch sometimes. There's shame and humiliation and a deep well of unworthiness attached to that voice. She's been harder to befriend, but worth it.

I recognize inner critic thoughts are a mixture of these two voices. It's a messed-up, complicated, chaotic stew of trauma that took decades to unravel. I dedicated my life to that healing journey. That commitment served me well and brought rewards (and challenges) I never imagined. Because once you're aware, you can't go back.

The first step for me was awareness. Awareness is everything. With awareness, we have a choice.

I started asking myself a lot of questions that you can ask, too:

Where do these inner critic voices come from?
Who said that to me?
What exactly did they say?
What did I make that mean?
How did I react?
How long have I been holding on to these unhelpful (sometimes paralyzing) messages?
How quickly can I call them out?
Do you believe everything you think?
What are you telling yourself every day?
Do you believe in yourself?

When we start noticing our thoughts, and especially the self-sabotaging talk that becomes a regular part of our day, we have an opportunity to change everything. What if you decide right now that you'll only speak to yourself with words that encourage, uplift, inspire, and empower, just like you'd do for a good friend, mentee, or child? The transformation begins now.

In 2016, Brave Healer Productions was born. It was a pivotal *and* traumatic year. I asked for a divorce and labeled that year "the worst of my life" until January 26, 2020. The story about my daughter and our four-year fight to put her abuser in prison began that year. You can read some of it in the book *Love Warriors*. Oddly enough, the beginning of 2020 was also what I considered the catapult of the Brave Healer empire and the purposeful work that ended up being a survival strategy as I navigated the justice system. Of course, it was also the beginning of the pandemic.

I bought myself three divorce presents—my shadow black 2016 Mustang eco-boost convertible, fake boobs, and a writing retreat in Montana, not necessarily in that order.

About the car: The ink wasn't dry on the divorce papers, y'all. Her name is Jamie (as in The Bionic Woman, Jamie Sommers). Note: my hearing is bad due to multiple ear infections (and seven surgeries). It's a bit ironic, considering Jamie Sommers had a bionic ear. Did you know that the ears in Chinese medicine are about fear? *Huh, go figure.*

I was probably a race car driver in a past life. I bought that car, modified it to race, took it to the Maryland International Raceway, and ran the quarter-mile track twice.

I flipped the silver switch on the dash to Track Mode and saw the orange glow of the warning light. "Okay, now what?"

"Hold the brake down with your left foot," my friend Ben from the car club coached through my cell phone, "and just a little bit of gas with the right. Don't let up on the brake until the light turns green, then floor it."

I watched the SUV pull up into the lane on my right. *Who would race their Explorer? I got this!* I watched as the lights in the center turned red, then yellow, then green! I lifted my left foot off the brake and pressed the gas pedal to the floor.

Oh shit!

Yes, I beat the Explorer.

About the writer's retreat: I already mentioned it—the Haven Writer's Retreat—and you're all learning writing skills from me, thanks to Laura Munson. I went out to Montana twice to learn from her. She's the reason I teach writing the way I do. I emailed her that week:

"I just want you to know that I want to do this. I'm coming to learn everything I can so I can come home and do it, too." She welcomed me with open arms.

And, about the boobs: In April of 2024, I had my implants removed and reclaimed my body after eight years of post-divorce trauma, betrayal, and such a significant healing crisis that when I think about that woman, it's hard to imagine her being the current me.

The dealbreaker moment in my marriage occurred after an unexpected request from an acquaintance. He put my name down with his doctor as his emergency contact.

"Hey Laura, it's Stacey."

"Hey, Stacey, what's up?"

"C just had surgery, and he can't be left alone for the first 24 hours. He asked me to call you."

"Oh my goodness, please bring him over!"

The next call was to my husband.

"Hey, hon, how's everything?"

"Good, how are you?"

"Good, hey, listen, Stacey called, and C needs a place to stay while he's recovering from surgery, and. . . "

"No! He can't stay," I heard as he cut me off.

I ended up hanging up on my husband, who was away on business that week (a common thing). It was one of multiple times in our marriage where he refused to help people, and a lack of generosity flashed like a neon sign bolted to his forehead.

As I typed the last paragraph, I wrote with the awareness that my judgments about my ex are just that—judgments. I consider him to be one of my greatest teachers and feel much gratitude for that time in my life.

When have you shown up with a lack of generosity, Laura?

And—I was done.

My ex always assumed (incorrectly) that I cheated on him. C stayed in the house for a couple of nights after surgery until he could go home. We talked all night those two nights. I asked for a divorce a few days later and moved out of my home (where I both lived and worked) into a one-room studio two miles from the house because my ex refused to move during our legal separation. I came home at 5 a.m. every morning to help the kids get to school and start my work day. I left each evening to sleep by myself in the studio. I did that for almost a year. The story that led to all this? A much longer one.

C and I quickly became more than friends, and we've shared a life together for almost a decade now.

The fake boobs were a feeble attempt to feel worthy of someone younger than me—to be a woman someone like him would love, and a desperate move to be something I wasn't. It took eight years of healing, trauma, evolution, and more healing to make a decision to reclaim my body and have them removed. If there is such a thing as an eight-year healing crisis, I may have had one. I loved those girls at first but quickly realized they were too big.

"I'd like to be a C Cup," I told the doctor. The post-baby saggy Bs I had weren't living up to my 18-year-old mindset.

Afterward, I found myself having to buy triple-D bras. There's something very wrong about that. I'd educate any woman considering this option. There were so many questions I didn't ask and so much counseling I could've received to better inform that decision and shape a healthier outcome.

This is the first time I've written about this, but the second time I've shared the story. When I shared the stories out loud for the first time at our Brave Healer Writer's Retreat, I heard my inner critic louder and clearer than usual:

Martha: *Why are you sharing this? They're going to think you're...*

Me: *It's none of my business what they think! Hopefully, they love me for being me and for being brave enough to share my story. Hopefully, sharing it helps someone else be brave.*

Later that same day, in the cafeteria:

"Laura, that story you shared today? That was me, too. Thank you for sharing."

Our stories don't define us. They help us help people. Our mess, trauma, loss, chaos, or deepest joy becomes someone else's lifeline or path to worthiness. Judge as you will. I'm okay with that. What you think is none of my business.

Our stories and brave words aren't who we are; they help us understand who we're becoming or want to become. Sharing our stories is a portal of transformation. When we start that journey with courage, it usually ends with healing and becoming who we're meant to be.

I write and speak to Feng Shui my soul. I write to prioritize my healing first; it's my oxygen mask.

Your process—every experience, moment, sensation, journaled word—is a gift you get to shape and give yourself. You get to give each morsel of your own life its meaning through this awareness process.

With awareness, you get a choice to live your life and leave your legacy on your own terms. Your words change the world when you're brave enough to share them.

It's time to be brave!

I'm exceptionally honored and grateful to be playing in this sandbox with all the Brave Healers in this community, and to you for reading. The method of embodied expression I love to practice is called Brave Story Medicine™. I hope you'll dive in and feel everything!

The Strategy

The Brave Story Medicine™ Method
5 Steps to Sharing Words that Heal and Build Your Business

Essential preparation:

Ground and center yourself with five minutes of any kind of meditation or body awareness practice you enjoy that helps you arrive fully and gratefully in this generous, present moment (breathwork, sound healing, quietly sitting and clearing the mind, etc.).

Let go of everything else. Just feel. If you can't spare five minutes, then do three. No excuses.

Now, let's write and speak brave words. Here are the steps:

1. Journal about something that matters to you.
2. Read your words out loud to yourself or a trusted friend.
3. Write a story for others to read.
4. Publish your words.
5. Speak your words at a microphone.

There are no rules about the five steps above. If you feel any amount of fear, it will help to do them in order as they move from least vulnerable to most. Remember, your ability to show up with vulnerability is your strength.

Remember: Along with your expertise, it's your personal stories that make you someone your ideal client wants to hire. If up until now you've danced behind partial stories, the easier ones to tell, or self-sabotaging bullshit like, "Nobody wants to hear my story" or "My story isn't good (or bad) enough," get over it. This isn't about you. It's about the person whose life you're about to change. Be brave.

The first vulnerable writing you do is for your eyes only. Do not attach to the idea that anyone else is going to read it. Step 1 is about writing it for your own healing. Feng Shui your soul. Get it out. Be curious. Ask yourself: *Do I believe that? Is that what I think? Is that really my story?*

Let's do the steps.

1. **Journal about something that matters to you.**

   After you do the prep work above (don't skip that; it's a powerful portal to your inner voice and necessary), set a timer for five minutes, grab your notebook and pen, and write as fast as you can without censoring yourself. Don't worry about punctuation, grammar, or even finishing sentences. Just move what's in your heart, soul, and mind to the page. You can choose from the three prompts below or eventually do them all:

I feel _____.

What really matters to me right now is _____.

If there was nobody left to offend, upset, or disappoint, I would _____.

Feel free to make up your own prompts, write about what comes up for you, and/or something that feels like it wants to be expressed. Surprise yourself.

2. **Read your words out loud.**

   There's nothing more powerful than putting the vibration of your voice to your words and moving them from your heart to your tongue. Your *why* usually makes you cry. When you feel it, you know you have something others will feel. It's scary, but you've hit the mark when what you read reveals a part of your soul to you. Read your writing out loud to yourself, or to take things up a notch, read it to a trusted friend. Reflect on how it made you feel to do that.

   I know I have a story that'll resonate with others when my excitement or other emotion creates a change in my posture or the volume in my voice raises. What's your sign?

3. **Write for others to read.**

   In your business you write to communicate your stories in many ways—social posts, emails, newsletters, voice messages, etc. Try something low-pressure, like a social post. Share a story that helps readers and prospective clients get to know, love, and trust you. The more personal, the more universal. Don't cop out by stepping up to teach first. You'll always default to what's easier, and since we love teaching (telling others what to do), we tend to jump to that first. But who are you to tell me what to do when I don't even know you yet?

Let me get to know the real you. Be brave. Post your story and reflect on how it made you feel and what happens as a result of sharing it. Since this is a digital world, you can always delete it, which makes this process easier sometimes.

I have deleted social posts only twice in my life after I read what I wrote, and the energy of it wasn't something I wanted to attract more of. Everything is attraction. I take responsibility for what I share more often these days.

4. **Publish your words.**

   We're talking about a blog, website, book, magazine essay, etc. This is a bigger deal, right? More than your mom or BFF might read it. Yikes! By the way, that's purpose-driven fear you're feeling. It helps you know you're on the right track!

   For this assignment, choose a story that helps the reader get to know you better but also helps them understand the why behind what you do in the world and the legacy you want to leave. Your passion matters. And what's in this for the reader? What do they want that you're going to deliver?

   Everyone has a book in them. Stories heal—you, your readers, and your clients. If you want to write the book but feel paralyzed by that self-sabotaging inner critic BS again, pause and detach from the book being anything you'll publish. Just write it. Get it out. Then, later, you can decide what gets published. You can work with editors and coaches to refine it. No matter what your story is, there's a way to write it that leaves you feeling proud and brave, and that will help someone else change their life.

5. **Grab a microphone.**

   This is a serious up-level of Step 2. It's the vibration of your voice to your words but amplified through speakers (and your whole body). Do it while you shake. Practice.

That visceral, I'm-gonna-die sensation will ease over time. This isn't about you. This is about someone in the audience who needs to hear your words. It's about helping them change their life. It's a big-potatoes kind of therapeutic feeling to stand at a microphone and take up space with your voice. I highly recommend it to all who want to heal at another level. It's medicine.

My poet friends call it "open mic therapy." Reflect on how it makes you feel. Then, seek out opportunities to do it again.

Okay, so maybe you've tried a step or two above. Maybe you're a pro, and Step 5 is normal for you on a regular basis. My question is, what's that thing that you're still a little afraid to share? This might be the exact thing someone's waiting to read or hear, in the unique way only you can share it, that will change their life. And make sure to go read my friend Meridith's chapter about speaking. She's going to help you become a pro at this!

When I watch my fellow entrepreneurs share their stories, there's one thing I see most often—they're not getting personal. The more personal, the more universal. When I line up ten business coaches to decide who to hire, it's the one who shares themselves vulnerably who gets my attention and makes me know without a doubt that they're the coach for me.

What's next-level brave for you?

Laura Di Franco is the CEO of Brave Healer Productions, an award-winning publisher for holistic health and wellness professionals and those who serve them.

Read more about her in the About the Author section.

BraveHealer.com

Chapter 2

Dream it, Live it

Align Your Mindset for Unstoppable Business Success

Carrie Dahle

> *If I could do it all over again, I'd align my dreams with my mindset from the very beginning, ensuring every step moved me closer to the life I always imagined.*

My Story

How many times have you set exciting goals, only to watch them gather dust in the corners of your mind? Or didn't you dream of them because you didn't know you could? Are you tired of seeing your potential go to waste? Or do you need to know what potential you have?

I know that feeling all too well. I've been there many times. There's a solution.

Three pivotal moments taught me the undeniable power of manifestation—each a testament to what I could achieve and a promise of what's possible.

Willing or Manifesting?

I sat there on my eighth birthday, crunching on the bubble-gum-pink popcorn ball my mom lovingly made for my birthday party. My two best friends were beside me, engrossed in Footloose for the 100th time. My baby sister, Patti, kept trying to squish onto the couch with us, but I kept gently pushing her away, my frustration mounting, not really at her but at the imposter sitting next to me.

This is so embarrassing! I wonder if they can tell. Of course, they can tell; don't be so stupid. You can't pretend this one away. Please, please, please, make this nightmare go away.

"Mom! Can you please take Patti somewhere else? She won't leave us alone," I whined, my voice a mix of annoyance and desperation. As I nudged Patti aside, the real source of my irritation was painfully clear. It wasn't my little sister; it was the **fake** Cabbage Patch doll resting next to me, a stark reminder of what I didn't have.

All my friends had one, two, or even three real Cabbage Patch dolls, each with that distinctive button nose and the all-important stamp on the bottom, a mark of authenticity. Next to me sat a doll my mother crafted with skilled hands. She went to the fabric store, chose the perfect materials, and spent hours sewing it together. She made a sweet little dress, styled its hair into braids, and presented it to me with eyes shining with pride.

But to my keen eight-year-old eyes, it was a fraud. It lacked the signature nose and, most importantly, the authenticating stamp. It was an imposter in a world where authenticity ruled.

Will anyone notice if I go and hide her in my closet?

At the party, I smiled and murmured, "Thanks," holding back tears as I set the doll aside, praying my friends wouldn't notice. But, of course, they did.

Mom was excited after everyone left the party. "What do you think of her?"

Honestly, I was pretty bummed, but I didn't have the heart to tell her. So, I just smiled big and said, "She's great!" That meant I had to play with her, showing Mom how much I loved it. But you know what? It wasn't all bad. As I played, I started noticing the little things, like the fantastic details on her dress Mom put so much effort into. And her hair was way longer and cooler than the real deal. Plus, she fit perfectly into all the baby clothes my little sister couldn't wear anymore.

In the days following my birthday, amidst the quiet moments alone with the doll my mother made, I found a tender gratitude blossoming. Although it wasn't the Cabbage Patch doll I envisioned, it was crafted from her love and time. Holding my fake version, I felt a mix of appreciation and longing, grateful for my mother's efforts while my dreams of a genuine Cabbage Patch doll continued to dance in the corners of my mind. As weeks passed, my gratitude grew and mingled with a growing determination. I was resolute; I'd have a real Cabbage Patch doll, no matter what.

Alright, alright, she isn't so bad. But can't I have both? Can I like the version my mom made and still get one from the store?

Ignoring the whispers of doubt, I began to notice every commercial, point out each doll in the stores, and linger in the toy aisles, my resolve turning into a silent vow to make my dream a reality.

Back then, we didn't talk about manifesting as we do now. My mom used to say I had a knack for willing things into existence and always getting what I set my mind on.

One day, while out with my grandmother at Sears, she needed to check out some tools for my grandpa. This boring errand brought us dangerously close to the toy aisle. Seizing the moment, I asked to look at the toys. When she came to find me, I was there, standing in front of the Cabbage Patch dolls, detailing what made each special.

My grandma listened and casually asked, "Which one do you like the most?" I didn't hesitate, pointing to the blonde with green eyes and one adorable tooth, "Her, because she looks like me." She studied the doll and nodded, "All right, let's go."

My heart sank as we walked away, but she paused, looking back at me. "You really want that doll, don't you?"

"More than anything, Grandma!"

"Well, it's still a long way till Christmas," she mused.

"I know."

"If I buy it today, remember, it's your Christmas gift. It's not cheap," she reminded me, her voice soft yet serious.

I felt the excitement bubbling inside as my grandma considered the unexpected. Then she did it: She bought the doll, transforming an ordinary day into one I'd never forget. I did it: I willed a real Cabbage Patch doll into my life.

Dreams Guiding Destiny

The next time I felt the power of manifesting dreams into reality, I was no longer a child filled with simple desires. Now, I was a mother, and each afternoon brought a tightening in my chest as I tidied up the house and washed the day's adventures off my two young boys. The weight of anticipation grew heavier with each tick of the clock; my husband would be home soon, and I never knew which version of him I'd face. *Will he enter with roses, mistaking them for the key to my heart despite their scent sending me scrambling for Claritin? Or will the door slam, signaling another night of muffled curses and the thud of fists against walls?*

I always told myself, "Better the wall than me," yet part of me wished for a bruise tangible enough to justify an escape from this captive misery.

Amid these turbulent emotions, my mind often wandered to a more comforting place. I dreamed of a life with Jeff, my first love. His kindness and warmth were the stark opposite of my current reality. We ended things years ago in a whirl of youthful folly, yet I often wondered, what if?

Ironically, fate moved us to the town where Jeff now lived. Amidst the turmoil at home, I indulged in fantasies of serendipitously meeting him, imagining a parallel life filled with the love and peace absent from my current one.

Then, one chaotic afternoon, my husband stormed in, and the familiar pattern of anger unfolded.

"What's for dinner, and where are the boys?"

I seized the moment to escape under the guise of getting my older son to his soccer game.

"There is a plate covered with chicken and rice on the stove for you, and the boys are getting their gear together for Tyler's soccer game. We'll see you later."

Shortly after arriving at the game, and while I watched the team chase the ball in a swarm of other children, a familiar figure approached. My heart skipped. It was Jeff, and he wasn't alone; a young boy about Tyler's age clutched his hand.

Oh my God! What is he doing here?

My stomach churned with a cocktail of dread and longing. Here's the life I fantasized about, walking toward me! As I let my toddler down, who had no interest in the game, I watched as he toddled straight towards Jeff. I had no choice but to follow.

"Hello," I managed, my voice trembling.

"Hello," he replied, his eyes searching my face for recognition.

At that moment, I feared the worst: he wouldn't remember me, that my dreams were a self-inflicted taunt. "Do you remember me?" I asked, bracing myself.

"Of course I do. I was just unsure how you'd react," he confessed with a sheepish grin.

Relief washed over me, and we fell into an easy conversation, reconnecting as though the years apart had been mere days. We shared stories of our lives and our children, glossing over the pains and focusing on the present.

When it was time to part, I felt a bittersweet pang, unsure if our paths would cross again. Yet, something inside me shifted. His reappearance aligned with my desires and what I knew I deserved. It seemed more than coincidence; it was a sign of my power—my own power to bring about change.

Empowered, I started transforming my daily routine. I would no longer cower at the sound of the door; instead, I filled my days with joyous activities with my boys, avoiding the dark cloud of my husband's moods. We explored parks and visited friends, and I found solace in the laughter and love of my children. I found gratitude for all the good in my life, and I began journaling about the life I dreamed of.

There were still plenty of tough days when I felt trapped by my choices, days when I doubted I deserved anything better. But those were the days I needed to dream the most. I clung to gratitude for the good things and envisioned a joy-filled life. Without those dreams and that bit of joy, I'd sink into misery, which wasn't fair to my boys.

Then, one sunny afternoon, as I walked up to the school to collect my eldest, there he was again, Jeff, standing casually by the flagpole. Our eyes met, and in that instant, I knew he was meant to be in my life again. How or when didn't matter; I manifested this encounter through my dreams, longing for a better life and being grateful for all I had. This was just the beginning of a new chapter filled with the promise of magic yet to unfold.

Aligning Dreams with Gratitude

Fast-forward again. Jeff and I did find our way into each other's lives. Over time, I exited my past life and built the life I dreamed of. With Jeff by my side in our newly blended family, I found the courage to return to a passion my previous relationship once dimmed: my dream of having a career and of being a success in real estate. This time, my approach was fired up with newfound enthusiasm.

Embarking on my journey into real estate wasn't just a career change but a declaration of independence from a past where my dreams weren't just deferred but deliberately shelved, left to collect dust in the corners of my life. For years, these dreams were silenced by a controlling marriage, where my aspirations were dismissed and my passions belittled. I was pushed into finance and bookkeeping, a field I loathed despite my burning interest in real estate, sparked by a mentor who saw my potential. Yet, every time I began to find my footing, get licensed, and start to build a career, we'd move again, uprooting my budding success.

However, everything changed when Jeff re-entered my life. He remembered the person I aspired to be, the writer and the real estate enthusiast, and encouraged me to pursue everything that brought me joy. With his support and the knowledge that all things are truly possible (thank you, Cabbage Patch doll), I was ready to dust off those shelved dreams and breathe life into them again. This was my first real venture into entrepreneurship, and this time, I wouldn't let it end in surrender. This time, I'd succeed, fueled by the encouragement to be everything I once hoped to be.

One day, a colleague in the industry caught me off guard with a question, "What's your goal this year? How many lives do you want to change?"

I hesitated, "Umm, I don't know. I haven't thought about that."

His puzzled look made it clear that having no goal was surprising. "Really? You should have a goal."

That evening, his words echoed in my mind. *What harm could setting a goal do? In fact, would setting a goal give me that much more of a chance to succeed?* I settled on the number 10. Ten people I would help find or sell their homes. It felt ambitious yet achievable, not quite one house a month but significant enough to be a challenge.

Around the same time, I revisited an old habit that always brought me immense joy: keeping a gratitude journal. But this time, my journal was different. After listing ten things I was grateful for, I wrote down ten things I wanted to manifest. This practice, though simple, turned out to be transformative.

Every day, I wrote, "I will sell ten homes this year." Despite not altering anything else in my routine, a shift occurred. I raised my energy level with gratitude and believed in my goals and ability to accomplish them. By September, not only was I on track to meet my goal, but I also realized I could surpass it. Energized by this possibility, I adjusted my daily affirmation to, "I will sell 12 homes this year." By year's end, I sold 13 homes.

The following year, armed with an understanding of why setting goals was crucial, I aimed higher: "I will sell 24 homes this year." To my delight, I reached this target ahead of schedule and closed the year with 36 sales.

I learned that the energy I put out is the energy I receive, and therefore, I could manifest anything when I aligned my mindset with my dreams.

Now, each year unfolds similarly. I set a number, write it down every day, and pair it with my gratitude practice. This combination of gratitude and focused intention harnesses a powerful energy that aligns with my goals, propelling me to achieve them year after year.

The Strategy

Now that you've seen how the combination of daily intentions and gratitude has transformed my life, you might wonder how you can cultivate this powerful synergy in your journey. Gratitude isn't just about feeling thankful; it's a strategy that can dramatically shift your mindset and amplify your ability to attract what you desire. By understanding and implementing these principles, you can prepare to unlock deeper fulfillment and success in any area of your life. Let's dive into how a profound appreciation of what you have can pave the way for what you'll receive.

Gratitude is far more than a simple thank you; it's a transformative tool that shifts your mindset, encourages positive thinking, and opens you up to the endless possibilities of what can be achieved. In my journey, embracing gratitude has been pivotal in attracting success and maintaining it over the long haul.

Starting with Gratitude

Begin each day by reflecting on ten things you are grateful for. This practice isn't just about feeling good; it sets the tone for a mindset rooted in abundance. By acknowledging the wealth of positivity already present in your life, you cultivate an attitude of abundance, which is crucial for successful manifestation. Focusing on what you have rather than your lack shifts your perspective to opportunity and possibility.

Manifesting Your Dreams

With a foundation of gratitude established, the next step is to define and write down ten specific things you aim to bring into your life. Writing these manifestations as if they've already occurred is crucial, telling the universe that they've happened and you fully deserve them. This act of setting clear, defined goals as accomplished facts is essential. Writing them down daily embeds these desires into your subconscious, constantly aligning your thoughts and actions with your objectives. This consistent focus motivates and drives you to take the necessary actions to turn these dreams into reality, reinforcing your belief that they are indeed possible and already unfolding.

The Role of Reflection

Regular reflection on your progress is key. Take time to review what you've written, celebrate the manifestations that have come to fruition, and consider how gratitude contributed to these achievements. This reflection is not just about tracking progress; it's about understanding and appreciating the journey. It encourages you to recognize even the smallest victories, reinforcing your commitment and keeping you engaged.

Why It Works

This approach is effective because it merges the power of positive thinking with tangible actions toward your goals. Starting your day with gratitude lays a groundwork of positivity and openness, setting you up to focus on and achieve specific aspirations. This potent combination of gratitude and targeted intentions doesn't just envision a future; it actively constructs it, ensuring your dreams don't just collect dust on the shelf but become vibrant realities.

If you're ready to stop dreaming and start living, contact me at Thrive Mindset. It could be your essential first step toward manifesting the life you've always imagined. With the strategies discussed in this chapter, and particularly through tools like the Thrive Mindset Gratitude Journal, you can begin to align your mindset for unstoppable business success. Remember, the life you dream of isn't just a fantasy; it can be your reality. Dream it. Live it. Start today.

Carrie Dahle, CEO of Thrive Mindset, seamlessly merges her prowess as a top-tier Real Estate Broker with her passion for women's wellness and business manifestation coaching. With an illustrious career in real estate, Carrie has perfected the art of turning housing dreams into reality. Her transition into coaching marks a pivotal extension of her expertise, where she now empowers women to manifest success in their careers and across all aspects of their lives.

Carrie's unique blend of practical business acumen and transformative life coaching is the cornerstone of Thrive Mindset. Her offerings, from gratitude journals and intentional planners to life-changing courses, groups, and retreats, are designed to foster a balance between professional achievements and personal fulfillment. These resources are not just tools but pathways to a life where career success and personal wellness intertwine, leading to a more satisfying existence.

Carrie's commitment to holistic growth is evident in her use of real estate principles to teach manifestation and abundance. She demonstrates that the skills vital for business excellence are equally crucial for personal enrichment. Her guidance encourages women to envision and create a life where their professional ambitions and personal well-being are aligned and interwoven, reinforcing her expertise and the benefits of her coaching.

Join Carrie on a transformative journey where she coaches and lives the philosophy of a Thrive Mindset. Here, success is not measured by transactions or accolades but by the depth of joy and fulfillment in your everyday life. Follow Carrie as she leads by example, showing that the path to true success is paved with gratitude, intention, and commitment to growth.

Connect with Carrie:

Website: https://www.thrivemindset.io
LinkedIn: https://www.linkedin.com/in/carriedahle/
Facebook: https://www.facebook.com/thrivemindsetpodcast
Instagram: https://www.Instagram.com/carriedahlesthrivemindset
YouTube: https://www.youtube.com/@thrivemindsetpodcast

Chapter 3

Your Vision Audit

The Missing Link to an Unshakable Foundation for Business Success

Sandy Travis Bildahl

> *If your vision is out of alignment, you won't get to the future on time.*
>
> *Fear stops you from achieving greatness. But create a brave, bold, and expansive view of the future, and your journey to success becomes unstoppable. Your brave vision weaves the present with the boundless potential of the future, pulling you toward everything you've ever dreamed of with passion and power and the freedom to be who you've always wanted to be.*

My Story

If you have a business plan, get rid of it.

I don't like this! My brain lit up with warning signs. *Stop. Turn around.*

As mountain roads go, this one was an endless experience of *up*. Dizzying hairpin turns on narrow rocky ground raised the altitude of my stress.

Is this high-alert trembling in my hands a sign?

I'd never been on a road like this before. Reality didn't look the same as the scenic images I imagined at home. I had to do something.

Rolling down the car window, I checked the facts. Crumbling gravel churning under the wheels sounded like building demolitions in TV movies. *Dust and destruction on my vacation?*

The white do-not-cross line on the edge of the road next to what felt like a 2000-foot drop to infinity was missing or faded. Exposed tree roots dangled midair. *Is the foundation below us questionable?*

My son, Travis, drove. This trip was his idea. "Hey Mom, want to go on a six-week camping trip?" was an invitation I immediately turned down. I never camped in my life. Could I see myself as a camping-by-the-side-of-the-road devotee? Could he? Had he imagined his mother falling into a deep, dark ravine? Should I have known better when I RSVP'd yes?

Right then, his view was middle-of-the-road safe. Mine was not. I decided to do a driver competency test and check his focus. Calm. Attentive. Staring straight ahead. No evidence of flinching.

I, on the other hand, was a flinching wreck.

31 | The Missing Link to an Unshakable Foundation for Business Success

"You're getting too close. Can't you drive further to the left?" was my quick backseat driver's direction, said with shrill desperation, a tone I wanted to avoid.

To distract myself I thought about the yes that placed me here now. After my first no, I used my expert skill of rationalization and decided this would be the ultimate business trip, where I could check out my philosophy that bravery becomes you. I hoped to test my bravery (the challenge was real), look at my fear (a 24-hour chatterbox), and create a new way of being me. *What was I thinking? Was this the Brave Zone picture I wanted?*

And now? Old me wanted that comfort zone. Yes, I wanted to escape reality. Retreating and going home sounded like a ticket to happiness. *The old me is fine*, I chanted to myself. But was it?

Remember Sandy? Oh yeah. Maybe the car rocking back and forth, which felt like severe plane turbulence, put my brain on hold. Before this trip (that would become a line in the sand, my life before and after), I found myself stuck and overwhelmed, with no idea what to do. The one bright note was my entry into the entrepreneur arena, with success coaching at the core of my business. I loved that. But what I hadn't counted on was the unbelievably busy, take-over-my-life details of business-as-usual (marketing, social media, networking, and on and on and on and on and on).

And so, I lost sight of one essential key to success. I forgot me. My vision of who I wanted to be was the foundation of my business, and I was crumbling.

Hello, hello, anyone home? No was my sad answer.

At home I worked like crazy, ready to give up, my teeth clenched with forced gratitude, trying my best to accept "one-step-in-front-of-the-other" tedium as a natural part of my business and my life.

But an as-is life was numbing. Planning for success was overwhelming. My eyes were heavy with lost passion. I couldn't see the future. And that's when Travis called with his invitation. Did he forget to mention the snakes, bears, and scorpions or the death-defying roads? With that thought, I snapped to attention. The old me had something to say.

"Could you drive to the center of the road? Please!"

"Mom, I know what I'm doing. Do you think I want to die?"

He had a point. *Could we die* was already rattling around in my mental survival kit. Could he hear my *please, please, please, let's not go over the edge* mantra?

For a moment, I reflected on getting ready for this trip. I was a good planner, and I liked that about myself. But we were traveling without an itinerary. I thought about how I spent hours preparing, researching, and thinking about this unknown travel style. *Was all that work useless? Where is the safety net of rules I counted on? Is making plans in the unknown possible?*

It was becoming clear that my brainstorming, solution-seeking, and hyper-focus weren't needed. Visualizing worst-case scenarios was on my strengths list test I just took at home for my business. I was good at scaring myself. Lucky me. *And why isn't Travis worried?*

And why wasn't he worried about my worry? A quick, "Mom, are you okay?" was all I got. Maybe he knew how to anticipate and ignore my fears because there was nothing to worry about. Was he right? Was I a scaredy cat with an overactive imagination? Was I afraid of fear? *Hello, Sandy; you might want to say yes.*

I took a quick break from my eagle eye, out the window sentry position, and looked over at Travis. He was humming. Relaxed. *Wait a minute. Hold on. My God, he just took his hands off the wheel to change the cassette* (yes, we had cassettes). It was one of a collection that ensured our 24-hour-a-day Grateful Dead serenade. *Just this once, couldn't we listen to the same song over and over again like we often did?*

33 | The Missing Link to an Unshakable Foundation for Business Success

I silently pleaded, *please, please, put both hands on the wheel.* He did.

The car tipped over a rock. I jolted to sitting up, ready. Leaning to the left, hoping I could affect gravity while gripping the seat, was dramatic and ineffective.

I looked down at my clenched fist holding tight, locked on the handle, ready to throw open the door and grab onto a tree. *Or maybe I could just jump out the window, or what about we just turn the car around and go down instead of up? What kind of world is this? Where are the guard rails?*

Where are the utility crews who would condemn this highway?

I wasn't used to trusting that everything would be okay without evidence. And why was Travis getting out of the car to move giant rocks out of the way? "Hey, what are you doing? Don't leave me alone on this slanted hill. Did you put the emergency brake on?" Smart right? Always thinking.

Okay. How many rocks can he move when the entire vista ahead is nothing but what looked like giant boulders?

My fear was exhausting, and this wasn't over. The car was still rocking back and forth. I tried to sound nonchalant and asked, "Travis. Do you think people ever drive over the edge?"

He just stared back. I'm guessing he had enough. But alert! Another car was coming around the corner. My adamant plea, *they've got to turn around,* disappeared in the breeze. We were going forward, no matter what. Bumper next to bumper, edging ahead in a dance of danger inch by inch, meant we were getting closer to the white line that disappeared under the tires. What could I do? I tried an old favorite. I cried.

"Travis, I can't bear to watch."

His answer was ready. "Just close your eyes."

How easy was that? It worked. Danger softened, fear stopped talking (briefly), and I whispered under my breath, "Never again."

But never again wasn't over. There was lots more coming, and it was exactly what I needed. I was due for a vision correction. I was about to see clearly for the first time in my life. So, was my business trip a success? It was time to go home and find out.

How I look at the future changed on that bumpy road. Now, I know fear stops you from achieving greatness. But create a brave, bold, and expansive view of infinite possibility, and your journey to success becomes unstoppable. Your brave vision of the future weaves the present with boundless potential, pulling you toward everything you've ever dreamed of with passion and power.

Here are a few things I learned:

1. Planning doesn't matter if your vision isn't clear.

2. What you see is what you get.

3. If you look at life through the lens of fear, you'll see stop signs everywhere. When you look through the lens of bravery, you've got a green light to live fearless and free on your terms.

4. You can't know the outcome of anything.

5. Fear is always along for the ride. Just make sure bravery is the driver.

6. Planning will only get you so far. Thinking has limits.

7. If your vision is out of alignment, you won't get to the future on time.

8. Align your vision with what you want, not what you don't want.

9. Your vision needs a vision audit.

So take off those fear glasses; they don't look good on you. Set your sights with a big, bold, brave vision and vision audit, a combination that ensures you enjoy your future success every day.

The Strategy

Your Vision Audit

Got vision? Everyone's tuning into the power of visioning the future as the secret to creating business success. Top biz execs agree. Like Oprah, who said, "Create the highest, grandest vision possible for your life because you become what you believe."

Or Walt Disney, who said, "If you can dream it, you can do it."

And Steve Jobs, who said, "If you are working on something exciting that you really care about, you don't have to be pushed. The vision pulls you through."

They're on to something because it works when you do it right. And that means embracing a two-part process, your vision and a vision audit, a powerhouse duo that does two big things.

Visioning (creating a detailed, sensory-rich picture of your desired outcome of success) and its copilot, the vision audit, keep you energized, motivated, and determined to succeed, no matter what. Together, they solve the "visibility, how do I stand out, get attention, be unique, and offer one-of-a-kind value to the clients and customers I want to attract." This combo is your key to crushing the competition.

For entrepreneurs, this can make the difference between a business that thrives and one that merely survives. That's critical information when you find out that only 50 percent of entrepreneurs pass the five-year success mark.

I experienced the truth about visioning when I discovered that the lens of fear was directing my future with doubt, stress, and worry and interfering with my dreams. Switching to the lens of bravery made all things possible on my terms. How you see creates the future you get.

This is why your vision needs to be the number one first step in your entrepreneurial journey. Without it, business is just business. But add your own unique lens of what you really care about and see that you matter. You're the magic ingredient. You are the vision.

Add your vision audit and you've got an accountability buddy and a 24-hour-a-day inspirational support system. A vision audit makes success click and stick.

So, where to begin? How about a quick visit to Vision Land in case you've never been there?

Creating your vision means tapping into your imagination, passion, and what you value most to create a movie in your mind of your best life and love it. Directing your future with your intuition, wisdom, and insight works when you keep the experience free from the constraints of problem-solving, how-tos, and all those fears that can get in the way of success. Think of visioning as daydreaming the biggest dream you can conjure up and feel it like it's real.

Here's a short vision example.

Close your eyes. Breathe. Turn on your imagination. Travel to the future and see yourself at a moment in time when success was realized. Look back and marvel, revel, swim in a sea of appreciation and gratitude as you experience how you were true to your vision, no matter what. Success happened. See with feeling like you're really there. You might even smile.

Your vision is pure you. And the bliss you feel in your vision will shine and infuse your business operations with value, trust, and believability. Consider your own personal passion and truth impacting the world. How magnetic is that? A business with charisma? Nice!

That's Part One.

To secure your unshakable business foundation, let's activate your vision audit and connect the future to the present time.

Your bold, brave vision is about to become a living, breathing force that inspires action, drives innovation, and transforms your entrepreneurial journey into one of purpose, passion, and profound fulfillment.

Consider your audit bliss insurance that keeps your vision alive and well.

Think of your vision audit as a dashboard for your business—where your strategy for success comes equipped with a vision meter that measures and assesses how well your vision of the future is aligned with your values, direction, and focus. This instrument serves as your guide as you navigate the twists and turns of entrepreneurship, helping you stay on course toward your desired destination, which is your vision! What makes this work best? Picture each idea and question before you answer. Feel what's really true, not what you think is real.

Rate the following from 1 to 5 (5 is a big yes. 1 is close to no):

Values Check:

The vision meter begins by assessing alignment with your core values. Identify values that are a part of your business vision. How about authority, balance, integrity or compassion, boldness and community or creativity, growth and justice? Are your actions and decisions in harmony with what matters most to you? I'll send you a values list and template if you need guidance on choosing your top values.

Bravery vs. Fear Gauge:

Next, gauge whether you're viewing your business landscape through the lens of bravery or fear. Are you boldly pursuing opportunities, or is fear holding you back? Not sure? Use your visioning powers to imagine the outcome of doing what you want or not. Check out each option. When you see and feel the results, you'll know the answer.

Distraction Detector:

Keep an eye out for distractions that divert your attention like shiny new opportunities or unexpected challenges. Checking email and social media, running errands, shopping, and talking to friends on the phone count.

Course Correction Indicator:

If you find yourself veering off track, course-correct. What's needed to realign with your vision and values? What's missing? Your intuition knows. Need ideas? Close your eyes and turn on your imagination to come up with new solutions. Ask your inner intelligence for help. Think of it as inner brainstorming.

Progress Tracker:

Is your progress aligning with your vision and values so it evolves over time? Can you change, grow, and stay true to your vision? Make sure the actions you take are right for where you and your business are. The outside world has lots of suggestions that can influence action. It's better to follow your inner guidance, trust yourself and your own inner nudges.

Vision Audit Assessment Circle

Want to go deeper? Be more specific. Look at defined areas of your business. Check on satisfaction, happiness, productivity, and energy. The vision audit circle complements the vision meter, creating a detailed visual assessment.

- **Draw a circle:**

  To make it easy, I can send you one. Contact me for my vision and vision audit resource gift.

  Rate the following from 1 to 5 (5 is a big yes. 1 is close to no):

- **Center Point: Vision and Values:**

  At the center of the circle, note your business's vision and values. What do you see? What values are key? Rate where you are. Are your values clear? Check out my vision gift if you need guidance.

- **Spokes: Key Areas of Assessment:**

  Divide the vision circle into spokes, each representing key areas of your business, like culture, operations, marketing, customer service, and products you want to assess. You can also audit time management, stress, overwhelm, and employee satisfaction. There are many options. The choice is yours. Rate the level of alignment with your vision and values.

- **Assessment Points:**

  Add details to key areas. For example, in the marketing spoke, include messaging, branding, and customer engagement. Rate each one.

- **Analysis and Reflection:**

  Consider the completed vision circle to identify strengths and weaknesses in each spoke. Identify areas for improvement. What's out of balance?

Take time to write down what you see, what needs to become more aligned, and what is going well. Keep this for future reference.

Vision Assessment Joy

Daily check-in: Activate your vision with a morning audit check-in. Imagine the future that inspires you and then consider your day. Speaking at a meeting? Writing a report? Facing a tough sales call? Desperate for self-care time? Take a few minutes to see and feel the outcome of whatever you face as successful, energizing, and positive. Visioning is mental preparation. It's what athletes do before a game. It turns on the lens of bravery and the emotions of success before they happen.

And it works! When you begin your day with success on your mind, confidence, energy, and joy ignite everything you want to do.

Now if you're ready to start business planning, go for it. You have a strong foundation where your actions will turn into the success of your dreams!

I've got a gift for you! I've put together a Create Your Vision and Vision Audit Resource Kit.

Included are audio meditations, a values template, and a vision audit assessment circle.

And a bonus—enjoy a complimentary conversation with me to talk about visions, vision audits, and making meaningful, satisfying success happen! Copy and paste this link, and they'll be on their way to you:

https://braverybecomesyou.com/visiongift

Sandy Travis Bildahl is a certified business and emotional intelligence coach, motivational speaker, and creator of a life-changing system of personal transformation that awakens insight, vision, and the passion of bravery to design your unique, inspired life.

Her 30-year background as an entrepreneur and her extensive experience in different industries and organizations, both profit and not profit add a depth of understanding business strategy and structure to her coaching for entrepreneurs. Her passion is guiding and inspiring others to enjoy and create a meaningful, satisfying journey to success. She is also the creator of workshops that focus on archetypes, symbols, and stories that evoke creative thinking and imaginative problem-solving. Through visioning, exploring, and integrating inner and outer experience, new empowered options take shape, old patterns shift, and desired outcomes become real.

Stories have propelled Sandy's career from the start. Her award-winning work with Bob Keeshan (aka Captain Kangaroo) at the CBS Radio Network focused on interviews with hundreds of experts and personalities such as Jamie Lee Curtis, Buckminster Fuller, James Michener, Olivia DeHavilland, Debbie Reynolds, Judy Blume, Russell Baker, Joe Namath, and many more. Whether her work was in magazines, advertising, television, or radio, stories were the focus. Sandy currently lives in Annapolis, Maryland, where she is also an artist. She loves the wonder of adventure, being scared, and living brave.

Connect with Sandy:

Website: http://braverybecomesyou.com

Facebook: http://www.facebook.com/braverybecomesyou

Instagram: https://www.instagram.com/braverybecomesyou/

LinkedIn: https://www.linkedin.com/in/sandy-travis-bildahl-95309914/

The book *Bravery Becomes You: On the Road to Fearless and Free* is available at http://www.amazon.com/dp/B094GJG3LD

Chapter 4

Express Your Uniqueness
Secrets to a Jaw-Dropping Brand
Melissa Henry

> *Your uniqueness is the KEY to a jaw-dropping, client-attracting, business-building brand.*

My Story

If you don't know what makes you truly unique in your space, I promise that none of this entrepreneur stuff is going to work out for you.

"What's wrong with you?" shouted Patricia. "You said you'd have these on my desk by ten, and it's already 10:30."

I can't believe it's 10:00 PM, and she's shouting at me!

My cheeks flushed hot, and I felt like I was going to throw up.

"Don't you know what you're doing? You got the training; why can't you get this done faster?" More shouting.

Why won't she just shut up and leave me alone?

My hand balled itself into a tight fist, and I found myself in the midst of what I can only describe as a fight or flight moment: caught between wanting to grab my bag and flee the scene or spinning around to punch Patricia right in the face!

Thankfully, this moment of emotional abuse was cut short by the approach of Jennifer, the Division Chief, who swooped in to shoo Patricia away.

"Are you okay?" Jennifer asked.

"No, I am definitely *not* okay," I replied.

The entire situation on this project was *not okay*. But finding myself in what I considered at the time to be an impossible situation, I just sucked it up and kept going.

I was promoted to Project Manager, working for a certain (somewhat infamous) federal agency in Washington, DC. My desk was situated in a cube farm that felt like it stretched for miles in either direction. I was handed a team far too small and inexperienced and only one month to learn *everything* the previous contracting team had been doing for *years*.

Yep, one of those impossible situations I believe the Universe puts us in when it knows we're meant for much more.

For me, I felt exactly like a rat trapped in a cage—no way out!

During that time, my five-year-old daughter missed me terribly and cried a lot because I wasn't home to have dinner with her and her daddy or read her a book at bedtime. My husband slept on the couch every night until I got home to make sure I got home safely.

I remember at one point, he opened the door for me at 3 AM as I stepped out of an Uber, and asked, "What the Hell is going on at that place?"

Hot tears poured down my face as I said, "I don't know! I just don't know."

This sounds crazy to me as I write this, but even though the emotional abuse that was a part of the culture of that agency continued, I didn't find the courage to quit right away.

There was an internal dialogue that played like a favorite Spotify list in my mind:

I can't quit. We need my salary right now.

We just don't have enough saved yet for me to go full-time in my business.

Oh, and here's the one that seemed to play the loudest: *I don't know if I am good enough to be successful.*

The thing is, by the time I was placed on that impossible project, I'd wanted to go full-time in my photography business for eight years! I knew I wasn't following my true calling. That job was a means to an end, and I was good at it. I just didn't love it.

This waiting game went on for so long because deep down inside, I didn't know what made me different than any other photographer out there. I didn't know how I could create a unique brand so my business would succeed. I craved a sense of security and confidence: *If I take this huge risk, it better work out!*

A battle of wills raged inside my mind between the big vision I had for a life of more freedom and purpose and the imposter syndrome that reared its ugly head all too often.

Then, about six months into the project, while dropping my daughter off at school one morning, I ran into Mitchell, the father of one of my daughter's friends and a past client of mine.

"You look, um, really tired. Are you okay?"

Oh my God, is this written all over my face for the whole world to see?

"Um, no, I'm not okay," I blurted out.

"I'm exhausted, and I don't know if I can keep working at this job anymore, but I'm afraid if I leave, I won't be able to help support my family."

As Mitchell and I walked from the school to the metro together, I laid out the highlights of what was happening: all the emotional abuse, the long, exhausting nights virtually chained to a desk in a cubicle farm, the impossible deadlines and expectations, and too much time spent away from the ones I love.

As I summed up everything, Mitchell shared that he faced something very similar. He recounted his story about being in an impossible situation and how he decided to trust in his unique abilities and follow his true purpose.

"Because I was able to pinpoint what I do better than anyone else, I found the confidence to leave that soul-sucking job and trust that things would work out for me and my family. I'm so grateful I did because things worked out great for us.

"Melissa, you have a studio, you have clients, you have all the equipment, and you have a great service. Remember when you photographed my family? You have a special talent in the way you create images that show the true essence of your clients. What more do you think you need to just quit and do what you love already?"

At that moment, I suddenly "got it!" Here was someone, not a close friend or family member, who clearly saw what made me unique in my space.

As exhausted as I was, I got on the metro to the office with a newfound hope and a fire in my belly. I couldn't wait to call my husband to tell him everything and ask him his opinion about the one question I was afraid to utter out loud:

"Should I quit?"

I'm sure you can figure out what happened next. Still blows my mind that I've been out of that toxic world for over six years at the time of this writing. Since then, my business has grown beyond my "humble" photography beginnings into providing complete visual brand strategy services, but that very difficult time in my life helped me figure out something powerful.

My whole career was inauthentic to who I really was. I wasn't using my gifts and talents as I was meant to. I was just another cog in the machine.

Not knowing my uniqueness.

Not standing out.

Not making a difference in the world.

Here's the thing: you *cannot* create a truly impactful brand and business without understanding what makes you unique in your space. Without this knowledge, it's difficult to create offers, produce engaging social media content, write sales copy, create a stunning visual brand, or, ultimately, grow your business.

Your uniqueness is the *key* to a jaw-dropping, client-attracting, business-building brand. So, let's dig into what makes you unique right now!

The Strategy

One of the things that held me back for so long from taking the plunge into my big vision of creating my dream business was I didn't know what made me different from the host of other photographers out there. That's why the conversation with my friend on the way to the metro that day was so eye-opening for me.

One way to look at it is that your uniqueness, sometimes referred to as your unique selling proposition or USP, is a characteristic, method, perspective, talent, and/or skill you bring to the market that no one else can claim.

It's what makes you the right solution for your "perfect-fit" clients. Once you hit on what this is for you, things will never be the same, in a good way! So much confidence and clarity are derived from finding your uniqueness. It is **that** powerful.

The good news is that figuring this out for yourself can be done using a step-by-step process. So, get out a notebook and a pen, and let's get started.

Part 1 – Internal Assessment

The beginning of this process is a brain dump inventory of all the things that make you, you!

1. List all the skills and expertise you've developed over the years. Include on this list the accomplishments, certifications, education, and professional designations you have achieved.
2. Now list out all the things you love to do. What are your hobbies, activities, and passions in life?

3. Finally, what are your core personality traits? What parts of your personality do you feel make you so successful in your business and/or personal relationships?

Let's take a pause for just a moment and look over all the things you've just listed. How do you *feel* about your list? Doesn't it feel amazing to look at this inventory of all the wonderful characteristics, experiences, and achievements in your life?

Part 2 – External Assessment

Now, we want to shift gears to what the "outside" world experiences about us when it comes to our brand. In some ways, this can be even more illuminating than your internal assessment because most people cannot read the label on the outside of the bottle they are in!

While there are sometimes challenges to finding out what people think about your brand, it's way easier than you might believe. In fact, there are multiple sources for this information, often hiding right under your nose.

Here are some of the ways you can uncover what your audience thinks. I suggest picking one or two exercises from this list that you know will garner the most and best information and which can be executed fairly easily and quickly.

1. Gather your most recent testimonials from clients and comb through these to find the characteristics your clients say they love about you. When you find things that come up consistently, write those down on your brainstorm list.

2. Do you have transcripts from calls you have had with clients during which you have asked for feedback? You can easily mine these for valuable feedback by uploading the transcripts to Chat GPT and ask it to summarize your clients' comments about your services.

3. You can leverage surveys to your email list or followers on your favorite social media platform to uncover what your audience

perceives about your brand. To encourage more participation, consider offering the chance to win a valuable prize or offer a special free download when they complete their survey. Keep the survey brief and to the point and ask open-ended questions like: "What makes our brand stand out the most to you?"

4. Review your recent social media posts and take note of what people said about your brand in the comments. Pull up your reviews on LinkedIn and/or Google and look for what people say is different about you.

No matter what method you choose, you should begin to see patterns in the characteristics that you uncover. Keep this in mind for later when we begin to evaluate these gems we are mining.

Part 3 - Approach/Process/Method

While it's true that your clients don't necessarily care about *how* you get them to the result they want, sometimes what makes a brand truly stand out is a unique method, process, or approach.

You've seen examples of this with companies like Uber and Airbnb. They were "firsts" in their industries with new approaches to traditional ways of doing business in the local transportation and vacation rental markets.

Now, you might not have developed a brand new way of doing business, but the methodology or approach you created is uniquely your own. You should *own* that for all to see!

In this section, I encourage you to dive deep into how you provide your services to your clients. See if you can, through this journaling exercise, find the parts of the process you created that came from an intuitive knowing that it would create the best results for your clients.

If all else fails, I've included the below list of ways in which your brand may stand out in the market, which can be helpful if you're feeling stuck:

- Special delivery system (innovative approach)
- Unique technology (brand new or innovative)
- Unique methodology (counter-intuitive approach)
- Highest level of service (as compared to others in your space)
- Authority on a specific type of client (combination of expertise and experience)
- Authority in solving a specific type of problem (combination of process and expertise)
- How you make clients feel (personality characteristics and values)

Part 4: Evaluate and Choose

This is the fun part! By this point, you should have quite a list of characteristics you have identified in yourself, those that outside parties have told you about, and possibly a unique approach, method, or process you created in your business.

Go through this valuable data and highlight or circle the things that are related and/or form a pattern across all the exercises. Here's an example:

Let's say you have an innate ability to instantly see the big picture in someone's business and how all the little details come together to form that big picture (internal assessment).

Perhaps you've also been told by clients that they were impressed by how quickly you were able to set up flawless systems and processes for them (external assessment).

Not only that, you've established a repeatable method that allows you to pinpoint the areas of your client's business activities that need process and automation first (approach/process/method).

If all that is true, you've found a pattern of related characteristics that are clearly pointing in the direction of your uniqueness. By the way, you may end up with more than one thing, and that's fine. Of course, you'll need a way to decide which of those sets you apart the most.

Lucky for you, I have that covered, too!

For each uniqueness pattern you have identified, ask yourself the following questions:

- Is it STRONG?

    Is your uniqueness important to your ideal clients and something they'd value as a part of working with you? It doesn't do any good if you identify that your uniqueness is that you play piano while roller skating if your ideal client needs a Facebook Ads marketing strategy.

- Is it SPECIFIC?

    You want your uniqueness to be specific enough that it's recognizable and different from others in your space. For example, the fact that you "make great coffee" is way too general, but if you make "The World's Strongest Coffee" (example from Death Wish Coffee's uniqueness) *that* is specific.

- Is it DEFENSIBLE?

    This means, can someone else EASILY replicate your uniqueness in their brand? For example, if you help people overcome emotional issues related to money, having an accounting degree and a PhD in psychology makes you a perfect fit for your ideal clients. That's one uniqueness that would be difficult to replicate without years of study.

If you answered "yes" to these three questions, my friend, you have FOUND your uniqueness! If not, all is not lost. I want you to celebrate that you now have a database of characteristics that make up a pretty sweet picture of what you bring to the table.

Your next step is getting help to see what you're missing. This is very likely a classic case of not being able to see the forest for the trees. The good news is that I'm only a phone call away. I've helped hundreds of entrepreneurs find their secret sauce and I can help you do it too.

My Linktree is below and there's a link on that site to grab a call with me. If you mention the "Small Business Growth" book when you book your appointment, I'll know what you need.

Final thoughts

Maybe you're thinking, *what the heck can I do with my newly defined uniqueness anyway?*

Here's how you can put it to good use to grow your business:

- Change the way you network by including your uniqueness in your 30-second introduction
- Add your uniqueness to your website and social media profiles
- Create case studies to showcase how your uniqueness contributes to the transformations you have created for your clients
- Create content (blogs, videos, articles, social media posts) showcasing your expertise and unique perspectives
- Create branded images that highlight your uniqueness in a visual way

Speaking of branded images, take a moment to look at the front cover of the book you're holding. What does the image convey to you?

I created the cover image, "Galaxy Girl," for lead author Laura Di Franco. I captured the absolute essence of how Laura wants readers to feel because Laura knows what makes her brand unique.

Laura is an incredible visionary, someone who reaches for the stars and brings her community with her. My friend, *you* are one of those stars in that galaxy on the cover. Now it's time to find *your* uniqueness so you can create a jaw-dropping brand that *shines*!

Melissa Henry, Founder of Personal Brandtography™ Helluva Brand™, is an expert brand strategist who helps visionary entrepreneurs create a brand that looks like what their big vision FEELS like. She'll help you attract perfect new clients, achieve your next level of impact, and make more money.

With over 14 years as an entrepreneur, brand builder, and master photographer, Melissa has helped hundreds of entrepreneurs gain deep clarity about their businesses and brands and show up authentically as the highest version of themselves. Her approach is a necessary and powerful combination of brand foundation clarity, visual brand strategy, and custom imagery, which optimizes your business to help it grow and scale much faster. Melissa solves this complicated puzzle for you and your business with ease, sharing the pieces you're missing so your brand quickly becomes an empowering representation of the YOU who was born to change the world.

Melissa resides smack dab in the middle of Washington DC along with her smart and talented daughter, Elise, and her loving and incredibly supportive husband, Mike. She loves exploring new places, sampling delicious wine, and having deep, soulful conversations with good friends.

Connect with Melissa:

Website: https://www.helluva-brand.com/ or https://www.melissademple.com/gallery/

LinkedIn: https://www.linkedin.com/in/melissa-demple-henry/

You'll find all my newest goodies neatly nestled right in here: https://linktr.ee/helluvabrand

Chapter 5

Soulpreneurs Who Can Sell Are Changing the World

The Soulful Path to Success, Contribution, and Abundance

Ann Hession

> *Stop trying to build your business backward—trying to figure out your niche and marketing message when you haven't even had more than a handful of paying clients. It all starts with sales conversations—learn how to talk with interested people about what you do from the heart and with genuine curiosity. Not only will you get paying clients before you get all that other stuff figured out, but over time, they'll hand you a better marketing message than you would've ever created on your own. Start with sales; the rest will follow.*

My Story

Please don't wake up; please just sleep through this quick stop. Oh no, are they waking up?

It's late July 2007, and we're driving home to Rhode Island from my family reunion. We had a great day at the farm where my grandfather grew up. My husband and I are enjoying the sunny ride home, and our two girls are adorably sacked out in the back seat.

But then he starts to take the exit, "We have to get gas; we don't have enough to make it home." We pulled into a gas station and convenience store to get some gas—and the key word there is *some*. We both knew we didn't have enough money to fill the tank, but we could get enough to get us home.

Michael's getting the gas, and I'm hoping we'll be on our way quickly before they wake up, but then:

"Mama, where are we?" *Damn! Knew that was going to happen. Maybe they aren't hungry yet.*

Wishful thinking.

"Mama, can we get some food? I'm so hungry. Can we get a snack, please, please?"

My tired, frustrated mom brain wants to say: "You should've eaten while we were at the picnic, there was plenty of food." But really, what good will that do?

Instead, I smile and say, "No honey, I'm sorry, we can't get anything now, just wait until we get home." That's not the end of it. The pleading and, "I'm so hungry, please mama!" continue from both of them, but I keep calm and promise them we'll eat soon. What else can I say?

There's maybe $12 in the bank account, and wallets are empty, and we have to get gas. Michael and I look at each other, but there's nothing else we can do; we just need to get them home. We fed the kids that night; this is not a story of true destitution.

But the rest of the drive home the only thing I can think about, and what I can't stop shouting in my head, is: *I just had to choose between getting gas and feeding my kids.*

There are moments in life when it's divided into what it was like before that moment and what it's like after.

Moments of truth.

Moments of transformation.

Moments of rebellion.

Moments of choice.

This was one of mine. I didn't know it then, but it was when everything changed, and that's where it started.

Back then, I tried to make a living as an intuitive life coach and holistic healer, and I was failing.

This is when I finally shifted out of what I can now see was total denial, thinking that somehow if I was just good at what I did (I was), cared a lot (I did), and really really wanted to help people (of course), that would somehow get me clients.

I finally got it that *none* of that mattered. None of it was going to help anyone, least of all me and my family, if I didn't learn how to *sell* what I offered.

No amount of training, no amount of fabulous program creation, and no amount of free sessions to build skills would ever make a difference if I couldn't sell it.

And despite what the online gurus said, clients weren't just going to "show up" because I was "following my passion."

The only problem with this great revelation, this long-overdue light dawning, was that I kind of hated selling.

That's not remotely unusual. Most heart-based, purpose-led people, like coaches and healers, are so uncomfortable with the selling part that they avoid it every way they can.

And it's why most of them—over 80% in my personal estimation (and that's based on over 10,000 one-to-one conversations with healers and coaches in the last ten years) aren't making a living doing what they love.

And I was very much part of that 80% in 2007.

But that moment at the gas station was a moment of truth; it was a "This *has* to change!" moment, and it's when I finally decided that how I *felt* about sales didn't matter a rat's ass; I just had to *learn* it, or I might as well just pack it in and give up. And I was *not* going to do that.

So here's what I did instead:

I went and got a sales job.

I got a 100% commission-only sales job. I figured, *if I have to learn this sales stuff, I'm going to get paid to learn it.*

And if it's commission only, I will. I can't have another gas station moment.

I went all in on that job; I did the sales training they gave us as if my whole life depended on it. Over that first year, I got better and better at it and discovered things I loved about sales, like helping people solve their problems, finding out what matters to them, and helping them get what they want.

Then I got another sales job at Business Breakthroughs International, a company owned by marketing expert Chet Holmes and his partner Tony Robbins.

That was a whole other level I pushed myself to. I remember actually throwing up partway through the hiring process; it was intense. But I got through and became one of their top salespeople, and then I even became a coach for them.

Over those years, I learned a lot of valuable and truly wonderful ways to have sales conversations, things I still use today. I also learned some things I didn't like, some ways sales is sometimes taught that do *not* work for me, that aren't aligned with me and what I value.

And along the way, I developed my own sales process, heart-based, even downright *soulful* sales—the only way that really works for most people like you and me.

And because I went through all of that and learned how to sell, I have my own multi-six-figure business, doing the energy healing and coaching work I love. None of that could've happened if I didn't accept that *I had to learn to sell.*

For all the healers and coaches and soulpreneurs out there in the world, most of whom are "allergic" to sales just like I used to be, I like to think that the journey I just described was me taking one for the team.

Over all those years, I learned how to do sales in an authentic and soul-centered way that works, so you don't have to!

The Strategy

There's a boatload to learn about how to sell your amazing life-changing services or programs effectively and authentically, but I'm going to teach you one of the biggest mistakes you've been making, probably every time someone expressed any interest in what you do, or even just asked: "What do you do?"

And this simple mistake—which is so easy to change—killed your potential sales conversations before they even got started.

I promise, if you change even just this one thing, you'll see different results right away. You'll also feel more confident, comfortable, and connected to the other person instead of feeling awkward, not knowing what to say, and having the conversation end with, "Thanks for answering my questions," or, "I'll let you know if I want to find out more."

Instead, you'll have more conversations that end with, "Yes, let's do it. Here's my credit card. How soon can we start?"

Here's how:

You see, most people fall into a trap when someone asks what they do, or asks to find out more about it.

I even call it the **"Tell Me More Trap"**—and I promise you've fallen into it many times! I did that a lot before I figured all this out, and believe me, it hurt every time.

Here's how the Tell Me More Trap works:

You're talking with someone, having a nice person-to-person connection, and then, for whatever reason, what you do or offer comes up. Maybe they ask; maybe it just comes up some other way.

They seem interested, and then they say the magic words, the words you've been hoping someone will say. They say something like, "That's interesting; tell me more about it."

And your brain goes *Woo hoo, they're interested; they want to know more!*

And that's when you fall into the trap.

You tell them more.

I mean, they asked, right?

Yes, but if you take away nothing else from this, please take this—almost always the worst thing you can do when they say "Tell me more" is to jump in and start telling them more.

Here's why:

You don't know WHY they want to know more.

You don't know, out of all the things you could tell them, what would truly be of interest to them.

Think about it. If you're like me, you love what you do. I mean, you love it, you love everything about it, and you could talk about it for hours—how it works, how you learned it, the difference it made for you, and all the ways it's helped people.

This is one reason why, when most people get asked, "Tell me more," they fall into the trap of fire-hosing the other person with *way* too much information. You go on and on and on. And the other person's eyes kind of start to glaze over.

Tell the truth; you've done this, haven't you?

And it gets more awkward; you know you're losing them, and you think: *maybe if I tell them this other thing, that will help.* But it doesn't.

And finally, you just have to stop, and they say something like, "Thanks, that was interesting; I'll let you know if I want to know more." They don't; you pretty much guaranteed that. Or they might say, "I'll have to think about that."

And you're left thinking: *What happened? I thought they were interested!*

Argh, I hate sales!

Here's the problem. What you need to do when they ask is *not* tell them more.

Instead, you need *them* to tell *you* more.

You need to find out **why** they asked.

Sure, they could've asked because they do have a problem or issue they're wondering if you could help them with.

But they could also have asked because they were just being polite.

Or because they aren't interested in what you do at all, but they know someone who might be, and they want to find out a little more before considering connecting you with that person.

Or they might remember that their cousin's daughter said she was studying something that sounds like what you just said, and they're trying to figure out if it's the same thing.

Or they know something about this and think they might have a resource for you.

I could go on!

Those are five totally different reasons why someone might have asked to find out more about what you do, and they are **five completely different conversations.**

If you don't stop and find out **why** they asked (what they're actually interested in), you'll fall into the Tell Me More Trap *every time.*

So here's what you do instead—and it's so simple!

How to Avoid the Tell Me More Trap:

Remember, you need *them* to tell *you* more first, and you have to ask!

When they say, "That's interesting, tell me about that," all you need to say is:

"I'd love to! But first, let me ask, what interests you about it?"

Or

"I'd love to, but first, what got your attention about it?"

And then **listen.**

Here's a secret. Most people think selling their wonderful services requires them to have the perfect words to talk about what they do and how it works.

It's not true.

About 90% of sales is just asking questions and listening to the answers, and only maybe 10% is you telling them about what you do.

Isn't that good news? Doesn't that take the pressure off?

To excel at sales means asking questions, being genuinely curious and interested in the other person, finding out what's important to them, finding out what they want and what they're struggling with. Then, only when you do understand, and they get that you understand, can you offer them a solution that can help them get what they want.

When you have taken the time to find out what they want and need, connected with them, and shown you care, they will want to listen to the solution you offer.

Asking questions instead of fire-hosing changes the energy, too, and that matters so much.

Not only does asking questions (rather than sharing too much information) help you know what they're actually interested in, but it also changes you and how you're being in the conversation.

Here's what I mean:

When you're all focused on spouting out information without even knowing what the other person's interest is, you're stuck in your own head, self-conscious, in an energy of convincing, trying to get it right, and trying to make something happen.

There's no flow, and there's no connection. You and they will both know that.

But if you instead start by asking them what interests them, you immediately will feel your own energy and your own mind be more **grounded.** You'll experience being **engaged** with the other person instead of trapped in your own head and your own fears and concerns.

Asking the other person about what matters to them automatically makes you more connected, confident, and present.

And that will make your conversations way more effective and even more fun – yes, you can actually have fun doing sales!

There are several more steps to fully handling the Tell Me More Trap.

The most important step is the first one I just taught you. I promise if that's the only thing you change, you'll start to see different and better results right away.

But you want to master all of it, and I want to go deep into it so you can have amazing, powerful, connected, and totally aligned sales conversations that lead to many happy clients or customers!

I'm happy to provide you with the full training on how to beat the Tell Me More Trap every time. Go to my Book Resource Link (below), and get it for free as my gift. It's called **"Sales Conversation Secrets: Heart-Centered Sales Made Simple,"** and it's all yours!

In that training, I'll walk you through each step exactly, give you great suggestions for questions to ask at each part of the conversation, and even teach you my favorite way to invite people to work with you. It works so well, and it's so simple and authentic you will love it!

Just remember, asking questions is the key, and the most important one to start with when someone asks you to "tell them more" is:

"I'd love to! But first, let me ask, what interests you about it?"

And LISTEN.

Ann Hession is an intuitive healer, coach, speaker, and soulful sales expert. She helps healers, coaches, and soulpreneurs who have amazing gifts for the world but are "allergic" to sales and selling. She brings 30 years of experience in transformational healing, as well as her experience having personally sold millions of dollars of programs and services, to help heart-based business owners transform their relationship to sales. That shift is essential so you can confidently and easily grow your business without ever feeling fake, pushy, or salesy.

When she's not helping healers and soulpreneurs transform their inner game and discover how "selling" can feel as aligned and powerful as their healing or coaching work, she's most often found reveling in her flower garden in the summer, reading a good mystery in the hot tub in the winter, or traveling somewhere beautiful to continue her personal and professional growth. That's because she learned from her mom that learning and experiencing something new every day keeps your mind and heart young, vibrant, and alive to possibility!

Connect with Ann:

Website: https://soulpreneursuccesscode.com

Get "Sales Conversation Secrets: Heart-Centered Sales Made Simple": https://soulpreneursuccesscode.com/sales-conversation-secrets-2-2/

Facebook: https://www.facebook.com/ann.m.hession/

Instagram: https://www.instagram.com/soulpreneursuccesscode/

Pinterest: https://www.pinterest.com/HealerAesthetic/

Chapter 6

Process Systemization
Business Growth on Cruise Control
Pauline McGuirk Penedo

> *The role of a small business owner is noble, but it's often overlooked, not by our communities or our employees but by us, the small business warriors. When you are in the trenches, don't forget to look to your left and right. All the support you need is there; you just have to know how to ask for it.*

My Story

Transition from chaos to calm and rediscover the joy in your small business life. Just as neglecting your team and clients can leave them feeling undervalued and unappreciated, a lack of systemization in your business can leave you overwhelmed and chaotic. Create clarity and consistency, and watch your business become everything you envisioned through effective process systemization.

Sitting on my blue couch in my new family room, which my husband lovingly built, I experienced my first panic attack. After finishing a call to the bank and hanging up the phone, I felt an overwhelming urge to get up and run. My breathing became labored, and a tightness gripped me.

Am I having a panic attack? Oh my god, what do I do?

The instigator was my conversation with the bank about the sizable loan I'd taken to start my hair salon business. I invested in myself, my vision, and my destiny, and I had to make this work. However, the voice that often told me I was incapable seized this opportunity to make me feel like the venture was doomed to fail. Calming myself and activating my more rational side: *It will be fine! I got this,* and I began to settle down, and the panic attack subsided.

Shaking off the residue left behind from this panic attack, I took some deep breaths and went about my day. I didn't know it was trying to tell me I needed a plan to navigate the ensuing challenges. I had a business plan of about five pages, which was enough to secure the financing I needed from the bank and the premises I required to operate from. The rest of the vision was in my head, and naively, I figured as I needed it, it would just show up and guide my decisions.

My vision for my business was connected to how I wanted people to feel. What was important to me was the impact I and my future team would have on our clients in the short time they were in the salon. I wanted our clients to soak up the passion we felt for not just doing their hair but for serving them. I wanted to see smiling faces, laughter, and the cash drawer ringing as people flocked to us and happily handed over their hard-earned money. I smelled the fresh coffee served with a little treat, the unexpected one you get when you order a cup in a high-end cafe.

I was excited and knew how I wanted this new business to look and feel, but I hadn't documented the vision. I knew how my new salon would be designed and whether it was functional, but I wasn't yet equipped to have others see and understand what I was trying to achieve. If I wanted this to work, it was imperative that I could easily translate the experience I wanted to provide and how I envisioned it to the awesome team I was about to hire.

However, we don't know what we don't know, and at the time, I didn't know that a comprehensive documented plan would have relieved me from this panic attack. So, I went headfirst into opening my business, knowing there were challenges ahead but not truly understanding, without my blueprints, just how much harder this would be.

When I started the journey, my thinking was simple: *I'm a hairstylist, and owning a salon means doing hair; I'm equipped with hair techniques. All I must do next is sign a lease, print up some business cards, get my clients to follow me, and I'm now an entrepreneur. I'll get the key to my new place of work, walk in, and feel that I have arrived. Success is mine, and I'm free to do what I want, when I want, in the way I want.*

Boy, was I wrong! The work was only beginning.

Once I started my business, it didn't take long for me to realize I was a one-man show. I wore all the hats: answering the phone, booking appointments, maintaining the property, shopping for supplies, and doing hair to generate revenue. Freedom seemed to be slipping away rapidly.

I hired a receptionist and other stylists to help reduce my workload. However, I made the mistake of assigning tasks to my staff instead of establishing clear processes. This only added more responsibility and headaches. I was always available to everyone because I worked the longest hours, was the busiest stylist, sold the most products, and brought in the most money. All this while doing my best to create a sustainable, profitable business. Everyone came to me with questions; I believed they should've been able to answer for themselves. When I asked for their input, they responded, "You're the boss, so it's your call." With more staff came more questions, often distracting me from my clients and compromising the experience I tried to give them.

"Okay, guys, I'm outta here. Mind the baby."

"Mind the baby" was a term I always used when leaving the salon. I told the team to make sure to take care of things while I was away, using the analogy of minding a baby so nothing went wrong. They knew I was half-joking but also serious. I wanted to emphasize that there were tasks that needed to be done while I was away and that *they* had the responsibility.

I left early, hoping to battle the long weekend traffic before everyone else decided to escape up north into the wilderness. We had the privilege of being able to buy a cottage now that I was back to work full-time; however, the issue was how I could enjoy it and not have my business fall apart while I was gone.

"Ah, finally, we're here," I said, turning to my husband and giving him a sly grin. "We made it," I said as we took the final turn onto our lake road. It was as if all the stress melted away, and I could turn off work mode and click the chill-out button. I settled in and picked up my first refreshing gin and tonic when my cell phone rang!

Glancing over to see who it was, I took a deep breath and rolled my eyes toward my husband. "I'll be back," I said, setting my glass down and reaching for my cell phone on the coffee table I answered it, making my way toward somewhere quieter.

"Hey Pauline, sorry to bother you," my receptionist began. I could hear my stylist Johanna in the background, "But Jo did a client this afternoon, and she just called back!" We had an angry client who wasn't happy with her service and a stylist who wasn't happy that she wasn't happy. Triggered by my insecurities and hijacked by the fact this customer wanted a personal phone call from me, I now had to take time away from my relaxing weekend to deal with this situation personally. Trying to calm down, I asked, "What is our company's promise around this?" They didn't know or remember. In my heightened emotional state, I interpreted it as them not caring to remember, which just added to my frustration.

"Okay, here is what we will do." I immediately lunged into fix-it mode, as I had done many times over the last few years as the salon leader. I reiterated our promise. At that point, it struck me that it was the one in my head and not documented anywhere. I made a mental note to correct this upon my return. We managed the situation, and I wandered back into the living room. Returning to my gin, which was now warm, everyone had retired to their beds. I took a deep breath, hoping to get through the weekend without another phone call.

This was my reality, and it was exhausting. I needed to find a way to make this business run without my direct involvement. I realized I needed to step back from working in the business. Instead, I needed to focus on driving the business's vision forward and leading my team to work independently without constant oversight. I wondered why team members could not handle things themselves and didn't understand our company's promise, and I thought about the fact that I hadn't documented this promise, which, in the end, held me accountable.

The path forward is clear.

I discovered the power of processes and systems through trial and error.

The Strategy

What is a process? According to my systems business coach, Beverlee Rasmussen, author of *Small Business, Big Opportunity*, it's simply how we do things. Beverlee also emphasizes that problems usually stem from a missing or broken system, not from your staff. This promotes an environment of appreciation and positivity rather than judgment and blame. A well-documented process behind every aspect of the business gives clarity to the team and consistency to the brand.

I used to think that a process and a task were the same, but I've realized they're quite different. Assigning a task is more general, for example, "Answer the phone." However, without wrapping a process around answering the phone, the person doing it is only slightly better than an answering machine. A process embodies our purpose, goals, and approach. It may deviate from the specific task when necessary, but it always remains aligned with our intention for our customers' experience.

Process thinking doesn't have to be complicated. Let's look at a simple process designed to give our customers the most comfortable experience.

Looking at the experience from the client's perspective helped me grow my business into the profitable machine it was for 15 years.

For many of our clients, a trip to the salon was a relaxing escape from their busy lives. Our salon became a haven for those needing a break from a hectic workday, challenging relationships, or just the demands of family life. People came to us not just for a haircut but to feel seen, heard, and understood. That was our promise to them.

Navigating the end of this serene experience was crucial. One moment, clients were enjoying their time in the chair; the next, they were back to reality. Given our stylists' busy schedules, staying on time was essential. I developed a simple yet effective process using color-coded cards to ensure a seamless transition without disrupting the client's experience.

Here's how it worked:

- A **blue card** placed discreetly by the receptionist on the stylist's station signaled that the next client had arrived early, so there was no need to rush.
- A **black card** indicated that the next client was on time and everything was on schedule.
- A **red card** meant the stylist was behind schedule, the next client was here, and she was not happy.

This non-verbal system enabled our stylists to efficiently manage their time while maintaining the client's immersive experience. Our clients were aware of our schedule but never felt the impact. They always received our undivided attention. This simple process significantly enhanced their experience, making our clients feel valued and cared for.

This example illustrates how a simple process can profoundly impact your business's sustainability. Happy, repeat clients elevate your brand. Why not ensure the experience you offer is the best it can be? A well-thought-out, communicated process can help a small business thrive.

Let's explore how I can assist you in developing processes to elevate your brand, gain customer loyalty, and create a cohesive team. The by-product of creating process systemization is that your entrepreneurial journey becomes easier and more enjoyable. It gives you back your time and creates abundance through increased profitability.

Here are the four components of creating a process.

- Design it.
- Implement it.
- Maintain it.
- Disregard it.

Design
Identify what's missing or broken:

- Identify pain points: Reflect on what keeps you up at night. Write down your pain points and keep a journal to track them systematically, addressing each one step by step.

- Brainstorming sessions: Organize brainstorming sessions with the entire team, allowing creativity to flow without judgment and creating a safe space for ideas to emerge. Trust your team members and make them feel integral to the company.

- Adopt and implement the "YES AND" approach from coach Shirzad positive intelligence course. Encourage ideas without judgment by responding positively and constructively, such as, "Yes, and what I love about that is. . ." This helps to refine ideas collaboratively and build on them.

Implement
Document the process:

- What it is: Clearly define the process.

- What it addresses: Specify the issues or goals the process aims to address.

- How it works: Detail the step-by-step procedure.

- Who is responsible: Assign roles and responsibilities to team members.

- Distribute documentation: Provide the documented process to the entire team.

- Feedback and questions: Open the floor for final feedback and questions to ensure everyone understands and is clear on the process.

Maintain
Maintain and improve:

- Regular check-ins: Consistently monitor the process to ensure it's being followed.

- Staff meetings: Revisit the process during regular staff meetings to emphasize its importance.

- Adjustments: Be prepared to make necessary adjustments based on feedback and observations.

- Open to feedback: Listen to the team's reasons if the process is not working as expected and make improvements, revisiting the implementation step if needed.

Disregard

Review and eliminate:

- Eliminate ineffective processes: Regularly review and discard processes that no longer serve the team's or company's goals.

- Focus on what works: Concentrate efforts on processes that bring measurable results and align with the company's vision.

- Streamline operations: Simplify operations by removing redundant or unnecessary steps.

- Encourage innovation: Create space for new, more effective processes by letting go of outdated ones.

So why should processes matter to you? I think we now need to look at some very important reasons why your attention to creating and systemizing your processes will help you achieve the growth you desire. Processes aren't just a set of rules; they're the backbone of any successful business. They provide a clear path for every team member, ensuring they know their role and how to perform it. This leads to a streamlined, error-free environment where everyone works toward a common goal.

- **Efficiency**: Processes streamline operations by creating standard ways of doing things. This reduces the time spent on tasks and helps avoid redundancy, allowing small businesses to do more with less.

- **Consistency**: Processes ensure that regardless of which team member completes a task, it's done the same way. This consistency is key to maintaining quality, building a brand, and delivering on customer expectations.

- **Scalability**: Well-designed processes are scalable, meaning they can grow with the business. Processes that are too closely tied to the founder or a single employee can become bottlenecks as the business expands.

- **Accountability**: Processes create clear roles and responsibilities. Employees understand what is expected of them, and managers have a clear basis for performance evaluations.

- **Training**: With processes in place, it's easier to onboard new employees. They serve as a training tool that communicates how things are done, reducing the learning curve for new team members.

- **Risk Management**: Processes can help manage risk by ensuring that there are checks and balances in place. They can also ensure that there is continuity in the business operations in case key personnel are unavailable.

- **Focus**: Processes free up mental space and time for small business owners, allowing them to focus on strategy and growth rather than getting bogged down in daily operations.

In essence, processes allow small businesses to operate in a more organized and predictable manner, which can directly contribute to their success and sustainability.

Small businesses make up approximately 90% of businesses globally and are vital employers responsible for more than 50% of the world's workforce. Yet, 51% of small businesses fail within the first five years, a statistic I find unacceptable. When small businesses succeed, they nourish communities, fund college educations, enable family vacations, and so much more. Small businesses are the backbone of most communities, and implementing effective processes is vital to their success. As a Systems Business Coach, I can alleviate the time you're wasting wondering why your business isn't thriving and we can embark on this journey together, turning your vision into a thriving reality.

Want to discover more? Let's go.
https://littlehillcoaching.com/resources#ProcessSystemization
(Rasmussen, 2023)

Reference list: Rasmussen, B. (2023). *Small Business, Big Opportunity: Systematize Your Small Business, Create Personal Freedom, and Live the Entrepreneurial Dream.* Brookswood House Publishing. Retrieved from Apple Books (Apple).

Reference list: Shirzad, C. (n.d.). *Positive Intelligence.* Retrieved May 29, 2024, from https://www.positiveintelligence.com (World Bank).

My name is **Pauline McGuirk Penedo**, and I am from the lively city of Dublin, Ireland, however my family, all nine! of us together, immigrated to Ontario Canada on July16th, 1984. My professional journey has included being a licensed hair stylist and owning multiple salons. I am also proud to hold a black belt in Shotokan karate, which reflects my discipline and perseverance. As a lifelong learner, I'm always eager to grow, adapt, and embrace new challenges. My most outstanding achievement is being a mother to three incredible humans.

For 15 years, I operated my own small business, which taught me invaluable lessons. I have honed my leadership skills, learned to navigate, and overcome various challenges, and discovered the importance of addressing my weaknesses while leveraging my strengths. I deeply understand the roller coaster of emotions of being a small business owner—from the exhilarating highs of success to the stressful lows of uncertainty.

My mission is to empower you with the knowledge and tools I have gained through my experience. I aim to support you in creating robust processes and implementing functional systems that can streamline your operations. Creating clarity and consistency with your processes will give rise to a strong team culture. We can lower your stress levels and give you more time to focus on what truly brings you joy.

Understanding the life of a small business owner firsthand, I know how crucial it is to have a support system that helps you grow your business and nurtures your well-being. I want to help you create a balance that allows you to thrive professionally and personally. Together, we can transform your business, making it more efficient, resilient, and enjoyable to manage while ensuring we take care of you, the brave small business entrepreneur.

Connect with Pauline:

Website: www.littlehillcoaching.ca
https://littlehillcoaching.com/resources#ProcessSystemization

Coaching: https://www.systemsbusinesscoach.com/coach/pauline-penedo/

Instagram: https://www.instagram.com/paulinepenedo/

LinkedIn: https://www.linkedin.com/in/pauline-mcguirk-penedo-46827153/

Chapter 7

Reduce Your Tax Burden
When S Corporation Election is Right for Your Entity
Michelle M. Burke, CPA

> *If taxes seem easy, you're doing them wrong. Enlist the help of a tax professional early on to protect your business investment and alleviate your stress.*
>
> *Are you ready to elect S Corporation status and save $5,000, $10,000, or more in Social Security taxes annually? "Heck yes, I'm ready; tell me how!"*
>
> *Or are you concerned you might do it incorrectly and end up with the IRS knocking at your door?*

My Story

Standing on the bow of the catamaran, Susie inhaled deeply. The fresh February breeze from the trade winds filled her lungs. For the first time in a long time, she noticed how relaxed and genuinely at peace she felt. She saw the lush green hills of Tortola in the distance. Their first night anchored off Cooper Island was incredibly tranquil.

"Morning coffee's ready, dear," she heard Blake call up from below deck. Just as the orange glow of the sunrise was peeking up over the hills to the east, she heard light snoring from her daughter's quarter berth and not a peep from the grandkid's cabin.

After breakfast, they pulled anchor and set sail for Virgin Gorda. En route, to their delight, they spotted three bottlenose dolphins playing in their wake. They stopped to tie up to a buoy at the Baths, donned their swimwear and snorkel gear, and jumped in the crystal blue waters. So refreshing! The water was so clear. A giant sea turtle swam gracefully below her. She watched in awe. The color of the healthy coral and all the sea life was amazing. Their family vacation was turning into a dream come true.

That night in port, as Susie sipped on a cold mango daiquiri, she took a moment to reflect on how she got here. She recalled it as if it was yesterday and instantly felt the blood in her neck start to pulse. Nearly two and a half years ago, that dreadful call came from their tax accountant on October 15th, the last possible day to file their extended 2020 taxes.

"Susie, this is Allison calling to let you know that I need you and Blake to come into the office today to sign your returns and write a check to the IRS for $6,361."

"How much?" surely she didn't hear the amount correctly. She couldn't possibly owe that much in tax in addition to the estimates she already paid as her business didn't earn much during Covid, and Blake recently retired.

"$6,361, but don't panic!" Allison said casually.

Too late! We panicked. We're in the middle of buying our new retirement home out of state. We're cash-strapped with the down payment before selling the house. And now at the very last minute, we owe how much in taxes? Seriously, what the heck?

"We're not prepared to write a check for that amount without warning. What options do we have?" she sighed, exasperated.

"You could request a payment plan with the IRS, get a lower interest rate, and stop late payment penalties from being incurred. Or, you could talk to Margie, a tax specialist we work with, and see if she could file an election to make your business an S Corporation. That way, you probably wouldn't owe any tax at all. She has been doing these elections for several of our clients this year and has saved them so much money. What do you think?" Allison asked confidently.

"I think it sounds too good to be true and why am I just hearing about this? That said, if it's legal and not too risky, we're up for listening to what Margie recommends."

So they talked to Margie. She calmed their nerves as she explained everything.

"You can file an S Corporation election for the small business and make it retroactive to January 1st, 2020." Margie continued, saying she successfully got the IRS to approve the retroactive effective date for her other clients, given all the hardships of COVID-19.

"Susie's business is paying too much in Social Security taxes due to the employer and employee's share given how business income and expenses are reported on Schedule C of your Form 1040. This is why you owe so much in taxes." Margie helped them understand the details, including that S Corporations don't pay income taxes; instead, the net earnings flow through to the individual owner. She assured them this was all above board and nothing new or risky.

Susie still felt a pang in the pit of her stomach that would not go away.

After her reassurances, they agreed to move forward with Margie's plan. Margie said she'd file the election immediately and the returns soon afterward and let them know how much they would now owe the IRS (and the state) after the changes.

Susie sent Allison and Margie emails each month to find out when their late returns would be filed, but she got no response. Once Susie sent Margie money to file the S Corporation election, she didn't hear another word from Margie or Allison. Susie didn't know they were waiting to hear back from the IRS about the election first. She kept attempting to contact them to no avail. However, in late March 2022, Margie finally sent over their 2020 individual and 2020 S Corporation returns to be signed and e-filed. Although Margie still hadn't heard from the IRS whether or not they approved the S election, she said it was okay to go ahead and file as if they had. Susie could now see no tax due on the S Corporation return and just a mere $500 due to the IRS and the state for their individual taxes. Margie's plan saved them nearly $6,000 in taxes; therefore, her fee to do this seemed justified.

Just as Susie's stress level seemed to be coming back down to normal, the real tax nightmare began. She still felt uncomfortable about the whole thing and needed to get their 2021 taxes filed, too. She talked to her business advisor. He said he had just started working with a very talented tax accountant, and he suggested that she reach out to her to get a second opinion on the whole transaction. So Susie contacted me, and I agreed to review her tax documentation and returns to reassure her.

On the contrary, I called her back after my review with unexpected news.

"The filed S Corporation election will never be approved for several reasons", I explained to Susie. "Although filing an S Corporation election is a great tax strategy, it's not a right fit for your business. First, the election form was filed requesting an effective date of January 1, 2021, not the prior year, as needed. Second, and more importantly, your entity was a sole proprietorship, not an LLC, so it can't legally file for the S Corporation election."

I further explained that if the election was filed properly and her entity was an LLC, she'd still be in hot water because the S Corporation tax return would be at risk of an IRS audit. The reason was that no wages were paid to Susie as the business owner during the 2020 tax year. S Corporations require the owner to be paid a reasonable salary for services performed.

This was the actual reason Margie's plan was showing a $6,000 tax savings as no Social Security taxes were paid at all under her plan as compared to the original drafted individual returns Allison prepared with both employer and employee share of Social Security taxes and income taxes reflected.

What on earth does this all mean?

Susie was back to square one but worse off. She paid Margie the fee to file the election, and she still owed the 2020 tax plus a growing amount of interest and late filing fees. Additionally, she would have to amend the 2020 individual return and now file 2021 taxes not as an S Corporation meaning they'd probably owe taxes for 2021 as well. *What a mess.*

Susie quickly hired me to file their 2021 returns and straighten up the 2020 mess. On the bright side, when I ultimately amended their 2020 individual return, I discovered that Allison double-counted some of Susie's business revenues, which had increased her taxes, and improperly reported Blake's foreign pensions, so she missed out on capturing favorable foreign tax credits. In the end, Susie and Blake got money back from the IRS instead of owing tax, interest, and penalties with the 2020 amended return.

"This was the best decision we ever made," Susie said, finally smiling. "This experience taught me an important lesson. Don't make your decision on which accountants or tax advisors to work with based on advice from a friend or someone's neighbor. Do your research and choose your accounting and tax team based on good references and professional experience."

Taking another sip of her mango daiquiri, Susie quickly calmed down and settled back into the present moment.

Whew! What a relief, she thought.

She knew their individual and business taxes were being taken care of this year while she was taking her family on a once in a lifetime trip, one that most business owners only dream about!

The Strategy

I shared Susie's story to illustrate that sometimes, an S Corporation election isn't the best choice for your entity. Getting good, reliable advice is just as important. Suppose your tax accountant doesn't have experience making S Corporation elections. In that case, mistakes can and will happen that can lead to headaches to unwind or fix, often while the IRS starts sending you notices. Some tax preparers push you toward an S Corporation election without weighing the costs and benefits to your entity. My strategy below includes what questions you should ask yourself before making an S Corporation election.

Becoming more educated about S Corporations will stop the sleepless nights and help you enjoy a stress-free tax season. You too can take your family on vacation and feel confident your taxes are in good hands.

S Corporations have tax advantages making them a good choice for many small businesses.

The secrets to capturing tax savings from S Corporation elections are as follows:

1. Understanding what an S Corporation is,
2. Knowing what the benefits and costs are,
3. Knowing when to make the election, and
4. Determining if the election is the right fit for your entity.

An S Corporation is a tax designation that allows a company's profits to pass through to the owners' tax returns to be taxed there. Both forms of legal entities, corporations and limited liability companies (LLCs), can elect to be taxed as an S Corporation. A sole proprietorship cannot make an S Corporation election and must first register as a single-member LLC with the state. An S Corporation can only have up to 100 shareholders, only one class of stock, and shareholders must be U.S. citizens or permanent residents (or certain types of trusts).

There are costs and benefits to becoming an S Corporation. Often, your tax accountant only informs you of the benefits and forgoes telling you about the costs; I'm unique because I want you to understand whether it makes financial sense for you before moving forward with the election.

Benefits:

1. The main reason small businesses opt to be taxed as an S Corporation is to reduce the amount of self-employment taxes paid, also known as Social Security and Medicare, not necessarily to reduce the amount of income taxes paid. An LLC pays self-employment taxes on net profits, while S Corporation pays self-employment taxes on wages paid to the owner, and any remaining profits are not subject to self-employment taxes.

2. Shareholders of S Corporations report the flow-through of income and losses on their tax return. Shareholders are assessed tax at their individual income tax rates, which allows S Corporations to avoid double taxation on the business income.

3. Since S Corporations are either single-member LLCs or corporations, they provide liability protection to their shareholders.

Costs:

1. If you're currently doing business as a sole proprietorship, your Secretary of State website can explain how to become an LLC and what it costs, both as a one-time fee and an annual fee to get

started. Or consult a business attorney to help set up your entity to do business in your state.

2. An S Corporation files an annual Form 1120-S with the IRS, and since it's a flow-through entity, it means there's no income tax paid by the S Corporation; it's merely taxed once on your Form 1040. However, there is still a cost to prepare the S Corporation tax returns plus your individual tax returns. Reporting requirements are generally simpler for an LLC than an S Corporation, as a single-member LLC's income and expenses are reported on Schedule C of your individual return.

3. As an S Corporation owner working in the business, you must pay yourself a reasonable salary. You're then considered self-employed. Determining a reasonable wage in the eyes of the IRS is a separate topic for another day. For now, understand there's also a cost to hiring someone or a service to prepare and file your payroll.

4. Often S Corporation shareholders want to pay themselves a low salary and take all the earnings out as distributions. Besides being scrutinized by the IRS as to the right level of wages versus distributions, the one thing most tax accountants don't mention is that by reducing your salary, you're paying less over time to your Social Security retirement account. If you plan to receive the maximum Social Security upon retirement, think again! Or plan; if you pay less to Social Security, then one strategy is to put the money you save in Social Security taxes into a retirement fund (which may also be deductible for a win-win), so upon retirement, you'll have replaced your Social Security with this income stream.

5. If, before going into business for yourself, you've paid in sufficient lifetime Social Security to max out your Social Security in retirement, all the more reason to be an S Corporation and reduce your overall Social Security payments as additional payments are not increasing your future benefits.

S Corporation elections must be made within two and a half months from the first day of the tax year by filing a Form 2553 (Election as a Small Business Corporation) with the IRS to be effective for that full tax year.

A retroactive election can be made, but a valid reason for why it wasn't filed timely must satisfy the IRS requirements. Also note that if you weren't paying yourself a reasonable salary during that retroactive period, you would be putting yourself at greater risk of an audit.

How do you know if and when an S Corporation is right for your entity?

Here are **four questions you should be asking yourself** before electing to be taxed as an S Corporation:

1. Have you been in business for one to three years?
2. Do your gross revenues exceed $100,000?
3. Can you pay yourself a reasonable salary and still be profitable?
4. Is your net income (after deducting your salary) more than $20,000? It's this excess that you can take out as tax-free distributions wherein the tax savings lie. Therefore, if you're not profitable, the costs often outweigh the benefits.
5. Bonus question: what is your exit strategy? If you want to take your business public or raise equity financing, then a C Corporation might be a better fit than an S Corporation.

If you answered yes to the first four questions, there's a good chance making an S Corporation would be a good fit for you. Reach out to your tax accountant and ask if they work with S Corporations and are willing to do a cost-benefit analysis of your business to see if an S election is right for your entity today. If not right at the moment, keep these questions in mind and ask them again a year from now.

Michelle's mission is to support you and your business in pursuit of a happy, healthy, and fully balanced life. She is a certified public accountant, tax and business advisor, author, and empath. She spent 15 years working for the Big Four public accounting firms, providing tax and consulting services. She spent another 15 years in corporate America, last heading up a two-billion-dollar global company's tax department.

In 2020, she founded Health and Taxes, LLC to serve the business advisory needs of women-owned businesses and their owners to help them grow in sustainable, profitable ways and dramatically improve the owner's quality of life for the long term. Health and Taxes is a play on "death and taxes" as she understands that the business owner needs to focus not only on the health of the business but on the health of the owner as well. She is passionate about working with women business owners, especially in the health and wellness industry.

Michelle enjoys sailing with her husband on the Chesapeake Bay, watching Washington Capitals hockey games, playing with her two rescued cats, gardening, drinking clean wine, and traveling.

Connect with Michelle:

Website: https://healthandtaxes.net/

Instagram: @healthandtaxes

LinkedIn: https://www.linkedin.com/in/michelle-m-burke-0274795/

Chapter 8

Hyper-Focused Revenue Clarity

Build Your Compass and Business ATM for Consistent Cash Flow

Holly Jean Jackson, CEO, Revenue and Performance Consultant

> *Our thoughts and words create agreements and contracts with ourselves, our loved ones, and the universe. Money can hear your commitments and words. When you have a legacy and goals that do good in the world, money will hear you and flow into your life. When you commit to a lifestyle of generosity, how can anyone say no to you?*

My Story

When Fear Rocks Your Business

What the Hell am I doing?

You could lose everything—you might even go bankrupt.

Everything you worked so hard for is gone.

It's time to throw in the towel.

Get a job again.

The COVID-19 pandemic spread across the globe and the business world came to a staggering halt. Many of my clients either lost everything they built or stopped investing in growing their business. They spiraled into protection and survival mode.

My breath caught, my shoulders rose like locked-up blocks of stuck muscle and strain.

It felt like the path forward was impossible.

And I felt so much anger.

I worked hard to build my business, which grew exponentially before COVID-19. The lockdown was even worse in California, where other states were much more open.

Fuck this pandemic!

Fuck California for locking things down.

*The people I care about most are hurting so much. I know people are dying and sick, but this is **insane**!*

How do we survive and thrive when we can't be in a community together?

How can we grow without community and support?

As I looked at my dwindling finances, I felt trapped, like I was heading to a prison or Hell.

If I have to go back to corporate America to get a job that'll be like placing shackles on my soul.

I can't go back. It's not an option. I have to figure this out.

I reached out to my local chamber of commerce for support. I called my local business bank for help and aid.

No matter what I tried, I didn't qualify for any support.

I was at the end of my rope.

This only made me more furious. So many of my clients also fell through the cracks—*so much for the so-called small business owner support!*

It all felt so unfair.

I finally came across an option I could use—I could borrow against my IRA under the CARES Act.

Hallelujah! At least there's an option I can take action on.

As I evaluated this option, it felt like both a flood of relief *and* a lot of pressure.

This meant I would be betting on myself. It meant I could lose $65,000 of my hard-earned dollars for my future retirement.

It also meant I would be behind on my retirement nest egg, which felt like failing. It also meant I only had three years to repay that money while earning a higher income. I was also moving back to North Carolina and investing in growth for my business.

That's a lot!

I got on the phone and called Fidelity.

I remember feeling shame, embarrassment, and guilt as I took out $65,000 from my retirement to fund my life and business.

But as soon as I got off the phone, I felt relieved. I also felt a whole new level of unwavering faith and commitment to what I was building in my business.

Holly, girl, you've got this!

Let's write out a plan today. Let's use our business ATM. Let's connect with our past clients, past partners, biggest fans, and trusted business community.

We can figure this out. We will come out of this stronger, better, and more confident.

Let's do this!

But first, let's get hyper-focused.

Let's revisit our Life & Business Compass so we don't get stuck in a corner while we go big.

The Life & Business Compass is a strategy I created and implemented two years before the pandemic hit. When I regrouped and revisited my values, goals, and priorities after the pandemic, everything changed for the better. You, too, can come out of any challenge in your business, even the big ones.

The Strategy

The Life and Business Compass

Two years before the pandemic hit, I discovered something—business owners, consultants, speakers, and authors kept backing themselves into the same corner of busyness over and over again.

They'd say, "Holly, this is the best strategy ever, but I can't put it in place." Or "I love this new template and process but I don't know that I have the bandwidth to take action." Or "Everything I'm doing isn't working. I feel stuck, trapped, and limited, like this will never happen no matter what I do."

I found their struggles and pain so infuriating!

They were doing important work. Many of them were helping heal people who were in tremendous pain. Several were building world-changing communities, foundations, and nonprofits. Some were building a legacy they wanted to give their children and grandchildren.

These goals, talents, and gifts were going to waste. All because they didn't have the right tools to focus their energy, efforts, time, and inspiration.

I made it my goal to solve this problem forever. This is what birthed the *Life and Business Compass* tool.

How we do one thing is how we do everything.

None of the coaching or consulting work we do together will work if you are too busy to take action toward growth.

Never back yourself into the same corner again. Never build a business or career that's out of alignment with what matters most to you—your legacy.

Grab the The Life & Business Compass here: https://www.hollyjeanjackson.com/bravebusinessbook

The Life & Business Compass has three core foundations:

- Your five life priorities

- Your three quarterly business or career goals
- Your *big* motivating goal or legacy

Let's break these down, and then I'll explain what this has to do with money!

Because here's the secret and my pro ninja tip for you today—where your focus goes, energy flows. And when you're aligned with your legacy and mission, money flows! I want you to be so hyper-focused on your legacy and mission that money flows into every corner of what you do today.

Your Five Life Priorities

I want you to meditate, pray, and reflect. What are the five most important things in your life today?

Don't judge or test if you're living by them. Write down what comes up for you.

Then, I want you to write down what success would look like if you lived according to these priorities.

For example, if health is a priority:

- You work out five days a week
- Continue to improve your hip flexibility
- Eat nutritious and healthy meals
- Continue to learn and read more about healing your body and mind

I want your priorities to be hyper-focused, clear, and specific.

Then, take it a step further and check your calendar. Are you living according to these priorities? Or are you letting busyness or others' priorities dictate your schedule?

- I have a feeling many of you will find that you are living out of alignment.
- Don't feel ashamed and embarrassed. Knowing this is great news!
- Because this means you have *space* to open up your life and go after what's important today.
- You can start saying **no** to what's not on your compass.
- But first, we have to be crystal clear.

Your Three Quarterly Business or Career Goals

You can't do it all. But you can *have* it all. But only when you are hyper-focused on what that is.

I want you to choose three (only three) business goals for the next quarter.

And if you're having trouble narrowing it down, consider these questions:

- What **one** thing can I work on today that will make everything else easier, faster, and better?
- Where can I recreate and scale past success in my business today?
- Which shiny object will help me reach my financial *and* legacy goals?

We need to focus to succeed.

One mistake I've seen my clients make countless times is chasing shiny objects instead of repeating what they already know works. You already know what's working in your business. Why not set a goal to add more fuel to the fire there so that you can chase that next shiny object later?

Assess what's working and tie in one of your quarterly goals, then create systems, processes, and a team to help you scale and grow that.

Choose your three goals carefully. Make them Specific, Measurable, Actionable, Reasonable, and Tangible. SMART goals lead to successful results.

Stop leaving money on the table and leaking profit. Once you set your three goals, commit to them. Share them. And make sure your calendar is aligned to make them happen. Break them down into smaller, more tangible steps so that success is inevitable. This is how empires and billion-dollar companies are built.

And you can do this too.

Your BIG Motivating Factor, Spark, and Legacy

Now it's time for the *fun* part!

It's time to dream—and dream *big*!

Don't let anyone, yourself included, try to bring you down or dampen what you want or desire. Building a business takes unwavering, unshakeable faith in where you're headed.

I want to know what your inner spark and inspiration is deep inside you.

I want to know what your legacy is. What do you want to be remembered for?

And if you're not sure where to start, here are some questions to meditate and reflect on:

- When you die, what do you want your loved ones to say?
- What are your superpower gifts?
- What are you on this planet to do or heal?
- On your worst days, what motivates you to get up and get shit done?
- What drives you even when shit hits the fan or life throws you a curveball?

When you do this, no one can stop you. Once you tap into and tune into your calling, this puts you into a flow. When you use your compass to choose what you get to say yes to and what you get to say no to, life and business become easy.

You will find magic and miracles open up right before your eyes. You will be amazed.

When you're in alignment, you are magic.

You are magic.

How to Use Your Life and Business Compass

Now that you have your compass, it's time to use it.

There's nothing worse than attending an event, getting a nugget of wisdom, and never doing a damn thing about it. Your soul and intuition know you need this. So listen.

Do the work to create your compass, but don't stop there. Now that you have your compass, you want to use it as an advisor.

Anytime you decide how to spend your time, look at your compass:

- Is that commitment, task, activity, travel, thing, or person aligned to your compass?
- Will it help you reach your goals this quarter?
- Does it allow you to lean into living by your life priorities?
- Is it aligned with your legacy?

If the answer is yes, then you should say, "Hell yes!"

And if it's not a yes, you need to say no.

You need to say **no** to anything out of alignment with your compass.

When we say yes to something that's not aligned with our compass, we back ourselves into the corner of being busy.

Our compass helps us say no to the most important opportunities, people, and experiences. And these *will* help us achieve our goals and legacy.

Now that you know how powerful this tool is, here are some tangible ways you can use it as an anchor in your life:

- Print out copies of your compass.
- Place them in your office, on your fridge, and in your car where you see them.
- Share them with your family, business partners, accountability partners, masterminds, and support groups.
- Make it a screensaver on your phone and computer.
- Share it on social media.

When we speak and share what we're creating, it's powerful. Our thoughts and words create agreements and contracts with ourselves, our loved ones, and the universe. Money can hear your commitments and words.

When you have a legacy and goals that do good in the world, money will hear you and flow into your life.

When you commit to a lifestyle of generosity, how can anyone say no to you?

When you share your legacy and mission, that's enticing. People will want to work with you.

They will want to support you. They will want to help you achieve your vision.

And that's powerful.

We're stronger and better together. Lean into that.

Share your legacy in every sales call, referral partner conversation, coffee chat, and elevator encounter. And see what possibilities open up for you.

I can't wait to hear about the magic this creates in your life, marriage, family, business, community—and especially your finances.

About Holly Jean Jackson

I am Holly Jean Jackson, Revenue and Performance Consultant, Speaker, Podcast Host, Author, and founder of Business Builder Throw Down. My career spans technology to communications, organizational change, public relations, and content strategy.

I have dedicated over 12 years to helping business leaders get their groove back physically, mentally, and emotionally. I led a Local to Global Policy Initiative to influence future leaders' impact on communities. Fun Fact: I played in Carnegie Hall as first chair clarinet and am a black belt in karate.

In my Peak Performance Blueprint, I look at a holistic and logistical approach to success. After all, one can't have massive success in business without a life of equal or greater success.

Business owners hire me to master the art and science of real success because most lack direction, action, and results. So, I help define and design a business roadmap for impactful visibility, intentional profitability, and endless sustainability.

Bottom line: Without action, nothing changes, and if nothing changes, why do it?

Most are taking action….but they are not on the roadmap of success, and nothing is changing.

Some take action…but fail to ask for the sale and convert solid leads into clients.

Many see the rewards of running your own business as enticing, but the road to becoming a successful entrepreneur can be the biggest challenge you'll ever face. And we know this comes from your belief system. The result, you can't attract the right clients, push your revenue to the next level, and make a larger impact

You all deserve to start building your unstoppable, profitable business today.

Connect with Holly:

Websites:
https://hollyjeanjackson.com/

https://inspirationcontagion.com/

https://www.hollyjeanjackson.com/bravebusinessbook

LinkedIn: https://www.linkedin.com/in/hollyjjackson/

Facebook: https://www.facebook.com/hollyjeanjackson

Instagram: https://www.instagram.com/coachhollyjeanjackson/

Email at holly@hollyjeanjackson.com

YouTube:
https://www.youtube.com/channel/UC3ElvJLGqpJ2ThA9utJCqMg

Chapter 9

Permission Slips from the Universe
Authenticity to Attract the Right Clients
Susie Schaefer, Founder & CEO, Finish the Book Publishing

> *Transform your beliefs, be authentic, and step into your greatness.*

My Story

Authenticity is an overused, rah-rah, woo-woo, bullshit concept.

And it has the power to launch your business into the stratosphere.

I used to hide my woo-woo mystical gifts from the world. I painted myself into the box of "shoulds" to conform to what was expected and acceptable. It was only when I embraced my authenticity through sharing that I was a healer with the ability to intuitively channel messages and read tarot cards that my world completely shifted. And it shifted big time, by attracting clients and referral partners who were creative, spiritual, and embraced their authenticity in unique ways.

Before my transformation, the struggle was real. Consistency in my business was sporadic, which I believe reflected my own energy. Like a rollercoaster, I had ups and downs, with an abundance of clients some months, followed by months where I feared I wouldn't be able to pay the bills. I couldn't see it then, but looking back, I now understand that hiding my true self behind a mask of bootstrapping and "rubbing some dirt on it" was only creating more self-doubt and resistant energy to receiving what the Universe (God, Source, The Creator, whatever resonates with you) had in store for me.

I simply had to embrace my authenticity and get out of my own damn way.

Interestingly enough, a colleague of mine, who I thought was a friend but turned out to be a frenemy in disguise (thank you for being a *great* f-ing teacher), was the one who told me that my "woo-woo was the sexy factor" in my business, and what I brought to the table for the world of publishing was so unique and different that it was cool.

What?

Not only had that never occurred to me, but I had spent my entire life hiding my true self from others because I was afraid of being seen for who I was on the inside.

This insight changed everything. I embarked on a deep dive into my authenticity through more consistent meditation practice, personal readings, and dipping my toe into the water by offering free readings online. Soon, the requests started coming in, and little by little, I gained more confidence in my abilities with the help of some amazing testimonials and feedback that were instrumental to my moving forward.

The next step was to monetize readings on my website, continue to offer free readings as a gesture of gratitude for being a guest on someone's podcast, and use them as a complimentary bonus feature for sales and marketing.

While I actively merged my healing work with my business, more of the right kind of clients consistently showed up (with energy aligned with my own). The connection between publishing and spiritual readings created a ripple effect, which translated into more of the right clients requesting my services. This increase in clients gave me more time for learning and expanding my intuitive gifts and teaching workshops, and eventually led to being asked to read for groups in a variety of settings

What does *authenticity* actually mean, anyway?

I kept rummaging through the card catalog in my mind, digging up examples of people being authentic, and it came down to this as the common thread:

*Being truly authentic is allowing yourself to be who you **are** in this world and **how** you show up for others, regardless of expectations or outcomes.*

As an entrepreneur, you're likely looking to attract the right kind of client. You know, the ones you look forward to speaking with on Zoom; the ones you feel compelled to send a personal hand-written note or a cute gift through Amazon; the ones who are grateful for the service you provide and pay their invoices on time; the ones who become your *friends*.

How do you attract those people?

Attracting the right clients is a combination of creating authenticity by setting the intention about who you wish to work with and doing the work on yourself. It's all about manifesting. That which we think about, we bring about. By identifying your ideal clients, you set your sights on what you wish to bring into your life; consequently, the work you do on yourself to become more authentic will allow the Universe to help those clients find you as you come into alignment with who you truly are.

It's kinda like magic. Awesome. Freaking. Magic.

Because **you**, the unique individual who meets their dragon in meditation, chants around a fire, has a meltdown in the presence of others, and steps up to be a seeker of truth and freedom; **you** are a sovereign being who has the potential to be truly authentic.

What is it that keeps you from being authentic in your life and your business, and what exactly does authenticity mean to you?

Let's explore with the intention of uncovering some golden nuggets. I'll reverse engineer this conversation by taking a closer look at authenticity, then unlock the secrets to weaving authenticity into your business to unleash your greatness and create an abundance of resources: money, time, and enough clients to create a waitlist for your services.

As words increase in popularity or become buzzwords in our ever-evolving consciousness, do they lose meaning, or do we simply need to reframe how we perceive the actual definition?

The American Heritage® Dictionary of the English Language, 5th Edition, defines authenticity as:

authenticity /ô"thĕn-tĭs′ĭ-tē/
noun

1. The quality or condition of being authentic, trustworthy, or genuine.
2. The quality of being authentic or of established authority for truth and correctness.
3. Genuineness; the quality of being genuine or not corrupted from the original.

Genuineness. Ah. That word strikes a chord in me. Being your true self in every aspect of your life is what creates a foundation for authenticity. Allowing yourself to be seen and heard as the unicorn in the herd, the black sheep in your family, or the woo-woo nut-job without giving a rat's ass about other peoples' opinions is precisely what I think of as being genuine.

At the healer's retreat, we tossed around the meaning of being "authentic" all week. By Saturday, the group was weary of the word, and it was beginning to lose its impact.

Without clearly defining how authenticity looks and feels for yourself, then you might as well pack up your shit and go work at Starbucks.

Of course, if working at Starbucks is your calling, then go for it with gusto and be the best damn barista you can be. But if you're an entrepreneur, and likely you are if you're reading this book, then you're being called for a higher purpose, one that serves others through a personal mission.

By defining what authenticity meant for me and bringing my woo-woo persona into my business, I could feel the shift. It was palpable. Now I was in the flow. I attribute the transformation in my business to my stepping into my authenticity completely and unapologetically. It shifted me out of the energy of staying small and hidden into expansiveness, which attracted ideal clients and referral partners, providing more stability, consistency, and abundance. In addition to fully embracing my spirituality, I published a mini-book about my divorce and leaving an abusive relationship. I could no longer hide behind a victim mentality and slapped on the armor of survivor to share my story with the world, which garnered an international book award.

Some of the tools I used while building my business and stepping into my authenticity include the following practices.

The Strategy

1. Create a **system of structure** that allows you more time to work on yourself and develop your authenticity. For example, I use an automated calendar system and have multiple links for complimentary consultations, readings at a variety of price points, and client meetings that can be used anytime. My calendar has boundaries with days and times that allow me to spend

uninterrupted time working on my business while giving me time off when needed to recharge, travel, or work on a project.

2. If there's something you avoid doing or simply is a time-suck, consider **automating that task** or hiring someone to do it for you. I'm a big fan of the "easy button" and where financial stuff used to give me anxiety, I now have an automated invoicing system that I control, and a back-end bookkeeper to work the details and provide financial reports. Easy-peasy.

3. When working with clients, I start with a template proposal, and then fine-tune it to meet their needs. This creates a custom offering for their publishing project while **staying within the boundaries** of what services I do and do not provide. This also gives the client a "white glove" style experience, so they don't have to fit into a pre-arranged package where they end up paying for services they don't need.

4. Create your **ideal client avatar**. Identify everything about them that you wish to embody in a client, down to the last detail. Give them a name. Does your avatar have a traditional 9-5 job, or are they an entrepreneur who uniquely serves others? Do everything in your business as if you're speaking directly to that avatar, and if it's a mismatch, it's gotta go.

5. Podcasts, speaking opportunities, and live interviews have been instrumental in boosting my confidence by sharing my back story, my transformative experience, and how I bring my unique healing modalities to the world. If you're considering hosting a podcast, start with being a guest on at least a couple dozen before making that commitment. I love simply **showing up for an engaging conversation** without the back-end tech and management of hosting.

6. Let go of the shoulda, coulda, woulda. Reflections on life are good for taking stock of your progress, but wallowing in "what could have been" is bad for business. Just like a relationship turned sour, you don't need to spend any energy on that low-vibration stuff. Learn from it and move on. Whether you realize it or not, there is **a lesson in there somewhere** for you. Be grateful and let it be.

These tools and practices gave me the time and space to release feelings of overwhelm and let go of my monkey mind by using my energy more efficiently to manifest what I wanted in life, including greater authenticity!

Look how far I've come.

Like the wind of a cool breeze on a summer day, my thoughts drift as I write, coasting amidst the leaves of the trees that yield to my wants and needs. Softly, the whisper of the evening comes, faintly as a nudge of some kind of change on the horizon. *What will happen?*

I take a deep breath. *And so it is.* We cannot steer against the change; it's already set in stone. The Universe's mechanism of fate and destiny unfolds before us like a cobblestone path.

What is it I fear? Fear of the unknown used to keep me paralyzed, and since stepping into being authentic, fear has lessened its hold on me. The thought of change now has me saying, "Bring it on!"

Over time, as fear dissipates, healing is an ongoing process. The Universe permitted me to move forward on my journey of spiritual evolution. A permission slip like those we used to receive in school, the anticipation and excitement of escaping the classroom to embark on a field trip to explore nature. We're granted free rein to soak up every moment of the great outdoors, basking in the scent of white jasmine and pine needles for just a moment longer before taking our dear-sweet-time returning to the big yellow bus.

Serenity. Peace. Deep knowing that I'm safe, protected, and free.

Accepting the woo-woo in my business brought me more consciously connected, authentic people who are living their purpose. But when things seemed daunting, mantras helped me get back on track; some of my favorites can take me from the depths of self-pity to flying high in no time:

- I fear nothing and let go of attachment to outcomes and expectations with a deep knowing that I'm exactly where I'm supposed to be.

- I am of the light. I come here to share my light and help others find theirs.

- My heart is big and there is always enough love for others.

- My purpose is to help others share their authenticity and step into their sovereignty.

- The foundation I have built for myself gives me the freedom to be myself.

- Other peoples' opinions of me are none of my business.

Laser-like focus: It works! When you're truly ready to step into authenticity, it requires showing up, being present, not apologizing for who you are, and stepping one thousand percent into this journey, not allowing anyone or anything to distract, detract, or derail you from the mission. You may find you need a little help along the way. Lean on your trusted guides, angels, and human colleagues to support you. The road to authenticity is paved with missteps, mistakes, and learning opportunities, which provide feedback for you to determine if you're on the right track or if you need to make slight adjustments. Being authentic also means fully accepting people as they show up, regardless of what they have going on or what space they are in. By not placing judgment or expectations on them, we allow everyone the space to be free.

Releasing attachment to outcomes and expectations opens the doors for exploring using a great exercise, which I learned from one of my soul teachers. Sit quietly with a pen/paper or journal at the ready. Write at the top of the page, "Wouldn't it be cool if_____." Then, after a few minutes of meditation, allow yourself to free-write (also known as automatic or subconscious writing) whatever comes. Don't think about it; simply allow the pen to move over the paper. Revisit your journaling occasionally and use this as a measure for where your intentions are being set.

You are the catalyst for change. You are the one, the high priestess in a deck of tarot cards, the seer through the mud and muck of life. You are the beauty within as we shed the construct created for us. Let us start anew and actively create the world we wish to be a part of.

All of you, embrace all of me, the wounds and the scars of the past. Then go forth and heal those things, wearing the scars like the armor of the Divine, for it is that armor that will serve as protection for myself and my tribe.

Our healing begins now. You have the strength and power within you to face the change that is to come. The permission slip is yours to behold. Step into your true authenticity, ring the bell, and your ideal clients will manifest one by one.

Embrace it.

Be it.

Revel in it.

Known as the Transformational Book Coach for Cause Publishing, **Susie Schaefer** helps her clients heal trauma through writing and intuitive channeled readings.

Re-awakening to her spiritual gifts later in life, Susie Schaefer is on a quest to help others clear negative patterns and heal generational trauma. When she embraced intuitive channeling and honed her "Clair" abilities, it became a resource for her publishing clients to overcome blocks and write from their hearts, not their heads.

Susie believes that books are the gateway to creating a movement. Whether writing a book helps an author heal past trauma or raise awareness for social change, Susie empowers storytellers to be part of the global conversation and create a ripple effect for humanity, particularly when an author shares their own story in connection to their mission, message, and community.

To learn more, visit https://www.finishthebookpublishing.com/

Susie is a bestselling author with multiple books to inspire others to be the change they wish to create in the world:

- *A Path to Purpose: Seven Inspired Stories to Discover Your True North*
- *The Pivot Project: Stories to Inspire the Shift in Your Life*
- *Your First Book: The Publishing Guide for New Authors*
- *The Escape: How to Leave Your Abusive Relationship Safely* (International Impact Book Award)

Chapter 10

Systems Success

Turn Your Job Into a Business that Runs Without You

Jonathan Probert

> *The way you do things in your business can change, but the fact that you're doing certain things over and over with positive results means you've achieved a certain level of success. So, instead of winging it, find what works, write everything down, and create a documented roadmap for growth for your business.*

My Story

Six months after I started my first "big-boy" job, I was miserable and knew it wasn't the right thing for me. Working for someone else was a downer, and I was inspired to start my own business.

I can't do this anymore.

The societal norm is to go to a university and get a good degree so you can go out into the world and get a good job. It's what all of my friends and I did. I think it's what most people do because it's normal—there's no frowning upon it. It's the standard, easy thing to do compared to building your own business in terms of making a living.

I chose computer science because I knew the money was good, and it was more interesting than some of the other things I could've picked at the time. I might have gone into some sort of engineering, but that requires a lot more math skills, and I didn't enjoy math. I also knew the job market was open. Software engineering is in high demand, and I knew any sector would have many open positions. It seemed like a reasonable path.

When I started the job, I felt excited. It was a big bank known for its good technology and software engineering program, and the salary was very good for a job straight out of college. Friends I knew went through the program and said good things.

My first (of two) rotations was initially not what I expected, but I was still starting out and hoped it would pick up.

I'll give this a few months; it's bound to get better.

Six months passed. And then another couple of months. I was still miserable.

I made it a year and was supposed to rotate to the second team. I hung on to the idea that the change would be the answer.

Maybe it's just the team that isn't that good. Or maybe it's the work that they do.

I rotated to the new team with hopes of it being better. It wasn't. It was the same feeling—a huge lack of fulfillment.

There wasn't one deal-breaker moment that first year. It was more of a consistent breakdown over time.

I can't stay here anymore. If I do, I'm going to hate everything. I'm done. I quit.

Working for myself may have been a better option from the get-go in terms of my time, freedom, and overall well-being. There was a sense of fulfillment lacking in my job; the feeling I was helping people was absent. Ultimately, getting support and the idea of building a business I believed would do well, help people, and become successful was key.

When it comes to my happiness, I realized it would be more than just what I did for a living that mattered. At the start of my job, everything was focused on the work and not much on me.

I realized quickly that I didn't have much outside of work, and work was miserable. I hated life. My mental health suffered a lot. I wasn't doing anything that made me happy, and if I was, it wasn't often enough.

To offset not feeling happy, I planned fun things for myself. I planned trips to visit my friends and go places together. I planned things solely for myself—a tattoo, getting a dog, and buying a motorcycle. I continued to plan these things out to have something to look forward to every month in hopes it would counteract the lack of purpose I felt every day at work.

Something has to change.

I enjoyed certain aspects of the field, and that focus helped me understand what I might be able to use to create a business.

The main thing I love about computer science is creating apps, scripts, or tools that get things done. I remember creating a program for my friends to enjoy music when we hung out together.

When we hang out in person, we often have Spotify playing in the background. I created a chatbot that takes a song and artist that you load into the chat in a certain way and the chatbot picks it up and cues it to Spotify. My friends and I could basically DJ for ourselves without having to go on anyone's phone. My friend Will hosts a New Year's Eve party for a group of our friends every year. One year I showed them the app.

"Hey guys, I made this app. Check it out. You can pick your songs and cue them up!"

"Oh, hey, cool. How do we do it? Show us!"

"Okay, put your song name in and now the artist name."

Whenever I bring the app up, in a matter of minutes, a few dozen songs are queued up from any of our friends who joined the fun. Every year, we have a few new faces at the party, and everyone enjoys playing DJ. It's a great way to get to know each other and enjoy a mutual passion—music.

When something is fun and easy, you want to use it more, you get better at it, and then things flow from there. I started enjoying creating apps that solve problems and looked for smart, repeatable processes that would help with other kinds of issues.

Then, I started talking to entrepreneurs like my mom, who had huge complaints about certain organizational aspects of their business. Her business was growing so fast that there were lists of hundreds of systems, processes, and procedures, and they were all over the place. We talked one day when she was frustrated.

"OMG, I can't find anything! Everything is everywhere! Nobody on my team knows where anything is, and I can't find it either! There has to be a better way to do this."

The idea we came up with was to create a centralized place to allow business owners to house their standard operating procedures (SOPs), give them an easy way to find what they need, and delegate tasks to their team of virtual assistants or other staff easily. This saves a huge amount of time. And time is money. For most business owners looking to grow past the first level (solopreneur) to having a team, creating an organized, indexed system is the only option for them to grow without going insane.

The alternative is trying to find things in a disorganized system of sites like Google Drive, Dropbox, or even your own computer. There's also the matter of sharing links and giving proper access to the team you're delegating to. When you can't remember where things are, or that's taking you several minutes each time, it's a huge time waster and stress creator.

Unless it's a very simple business whose operations don't require more than a couple of tasks, businesses generally need repeatable processes to be successful. That's why a standard operating procedure is called the effective standard for what you need to do. The more you grow, the more procedures there are.

If you have your collection of SOPs (your set of instructions), and they're disorganized, all over the place, and not easy to share with those who need them, it'll take up a whole bunch of unnecessary time, energy, and effort to do what you need to do. Instead, imagine looking in one place, clicking a button to share, and then it's down to minutes (seconds even), to get that whole process done and allow your employees to do the job they need to do.

"I'm worried, Bud. What if I'm sick and can't work one day? This is the worst thought I have about my business, that nobody knows all the steps or what to do, and my business will stop because I'm the only one who can make it run."

My mom's concern is valid. A true business can run without you. If your business can't run without you, you have a problem, and you've created a job for yourself.

"Let's get you organized, Mom, and create a business that can run without you. It will be a huge relief."

She agreed. We set off to create an indexed library of standard operating procedures for her business that allows her to have more fun doing the things she was meant to do in her business, allows the business to run without her when she's on vacation or just needs a day off, and allowed her to hire more team members and grow the business to the next level of success.

Now, let's talk more about SOPs!

The Strategy

I don't think standard operating procedures are a set-in-stone thing because the way you do things can change, but the fact that you're doing certain things over and over means they have a general (and effective) way of being done. So, instead of winging it every time you do it, find what works through trial and error, and then document everything!

See what the common factors are for each task you complete. If you're doing the same thing every time, note it down. When you come back the fifth, sixth, or seventh time, you know it's the right, smart process, and it gets it done quicker.

Then, if you don't want to do the particular task anymore, if it takes up too much of your time, and you find yourself working a job instead of building your business, you have this set of instructions to give to a virtual assistant or employee to get the task done for you so you can focus on other things.

Down the line, if your assistant says, "Hey, step two isn't working anymore. I found success doing this instead," you go back to the SOP, update it, and you have this new set of instructions you can move forward with. This is how your business grows. And it's how you build a business that can run without you.

To get a next-level handle on creating processes to enhance customer service (and the difference between a process and a task), make sure to go back to read Chapter 6!

Creating your task list is Step 1 to creating a business that can run without you. Let's get to it!

Your Business Task List

> **Step 1.** Make a list of every single task you do in your business.
>
> **Step 2.** Break your list down into your A list and your B list.

Everything you do in the name of organizing your business for next-level growth starts by making a list of tasks.

Open up a document on your computer. You'll start by making a master list of tasks that you do for your business.

Step 1. Make a list of every single task you do in your business.

Oooh, I know this may feel daunting, but the time and effort you spend making this list of tasks will be well worth it!

You might have bigger categories of tasks with smaller ones underneath them. The master list of tasks is your first step toward organizing everything in your business and setting it up for growth and success.

Step 2. Break your list down into your A list and your B list.

The A list is everything only *you* can do.

The B list is everything else—all the tasks you can delegate to someone else.

One of the biggest lessons I learned is that there were a lot more things on my A list that really belonged on the B list. Once I sorted that out, I started creating my SOPs and then began to organize them in a way that helped my daily flow and made delegating easy! I started to see the opportunities, including the "whos" I could hire to do each task.

If you haven't read the book *Who Not How*, I highly recommend it! It's finding the who's for your business and then giving them the proper access to your new library that will help you take it all to the next level, add that new program, or spend time with your bigger business vision.

Please visit https://systemssuccesspro.com for a free guide to creating easy SOPs!

Jonathan Probert is the CEO of Systems Success Pro and has a mission to help business owners save time, energy, and money with an easy way to organize repeatable systems that allow growth at the next level.

He's a University of Maryland Computer Science graduate and spent in a year in a junior software engineering role. After talking to his entrepreneur friends who struggled to organize a system of standard operating procedures, he realized he could solve a big problem and ventured into entrepreneurship.

Jonathan lives in Bethesda, Maryland, with his Staffordshire Bull Terrier, Bean. He loves video games like League of Legends and Valorant, going out with friends, eating Korean BBQ, and going to the gym.

Schedule a chat to start organizing your business systems today!

Connect with Jonathan:

Website: https://systemssuccesspro.com
Facebook: https://www.facebook.com/systemssuccesspro/
LinkedIn: https://www.linkedin.com/in/jonathan-probert/

Part 2
Business Strategies

Chapter 11

Digital Marketing Mastery
The Magic Behind Strategies that Work
Prati Kaufman, Entrepreneur, Marketing, and Human Energy Expert

> *The ability to say no to money, opportunities, growth, and people in the name of mental health and **decreased** stress is one of the reasons my business has grown so rapidly.*

My Story

I'm a child of God.

I can't pinpoint when I first embraced this belief, but I've often wondered, *who am I to think this?* Yet, how else can I explain my life, which is bigger than all my dreams? Everything I've read has become reality.

By conventional expectations, I should've been a teacher, lawyer, or doctor in India, married with three children. Instead, I'm an entrepreneur in America—a realm that once seemed as distant as the moon—thriving as a mother, wife, friend, and thought leader.

This is the journey and marketing strategy that propelled my business to a high six-figure success in just three years. Marketing strategy is one of the tools for business growth; it alone can't do much but is mighty when paired with a powerful mindset, strong team, and robust systems and processes.

I hope it inspires you to pursue your dreams, listen to your inner voice, and live authentically.

THE BEGINNING

As the youngest of three, I spent most of my time quietly daydreaming. Life was simple, perhaps too simple, even poor by Western standards. In hindsight, I had riches most people would kill for—a loving family, freedom to think, space to make mistakes, stories of powerful goddesses, and books to read—what else could one ask for?

Those riches made me fearless in a way only a naive teenager with no life experiences can be. Combined with the belief that everything always works out for the best, I took risks I had no business taking.

Imagine choosing to take exams in English (as a biology major in high school) even though everything was taught in Hindi in school. I spent hours translating what I learned on my own in English while other kids were playing outside. The Oxford Dictionary and I were inseparable.

Risks never felt like risks to me because they felt so right.

When I felt utterly defeated, lost, and broken, I had a loving home free of judgment to heal, always encouraged to follow my inner guidance.

THE MIDDLE

My inner voice led me on a path no one I knew walked, and I boldly said yes to every scary decision that just felt right.

Go to Dubai, the voice said.

I didn't question it. I knew the inner voice, intuition, divine guidance—whatever you call it—wasn't logical. It doesn't try to convince you; it's just there, loud and clear. You just have to trust it. Surrender to it. Trust me, I was scared every single time I took that leap of faith, but not doing so felt much riskier.

The fact that I knew no one in Dubai didn't matter because the universe lined up someone who could get me a visit visa for 15 days. I landed there with $100 and 15 days to get a job or go back home. I applied for 20 jobs daily and traveled on local buses in sweltering heat to get to interviews in a totally strange place. I had two nice outfits for interviews.

Of course, I got the job on the seventh day.

Whether I attended an English-speaking college without knowing how to speak English, started my career in marketing after a degree in hotel management, or moved to cities where I knew no one, every experience brought me closer to what I was meant to become. Every failure showed me the next move I needed to make.

The Universe will show you the next best thing. You just need to trust the process and let your faith be way bigger than the fears.

In 2019, when that voice said it was time to move on, I left a well-paying corporate job without knowing what next. With 20 years of marketing experience across small businesses and Fortune 500 companies globally, I was determined to leave marketing behind.

I decided to launch a community kitchen to bring different cultures and generations together through food. Leveraging what I learned, I spent nearly a year in market research—consulting restaurant owners, drafting business plans, scouting locations, listing necessary licenses, and engaging investors. However, I soon realized running a restaurant wasn't for me.

I just knew. Most of us may continue something because we have spent a year's worth of time and effort. But when leaving something makes you feel lighter and less burdened, you know it's the right decision. It felt like the next logical decision without the need for logical reasoning.

Things didn't go as planned, but the Universe had a different path ready. Small businesses sought my marketing expertise. A small business owner asked me to manage her social media, and when I asked what keywords were used on the website, she had no idea. It revealed a gap in integrated marketing services for them. This led me to become a marketing strategist to help them integrate their existing efforts to maximize the ROI. When a client needed a website, I admitted I couldn't code but could find someone who could. That client remains with me after three and a half years.

Since then, I've built a full-service digital marketing agency with a global team of 25, which is growing rapidly. My husband and I even recently acquired another business.

Before diving into the marketing strategies that fueled my success, let me share some mindset practices that were invaluable:

- Treating mistakes and failures as growth opportunities; they teach you what not to do.
- Avoiding labeling decisions as right or wrong; each one leads to the next.
- Trusting my inner voice, even when it doesn't make sense.

Here's the marketing strategy I've used for my own business (and for all my clients) to get in front of the right customers authentically and build a brand, trust, and credibility.

Research shows that people are inclined to buy from you after they spend seven hours around you, meet you in four places, and interact with you 11 times. This marketing strategy can help you achieve that and create a seamless customer experience across all platforms.

Disclaimer—For e-commerce clients, the same strategy will not work.

The Strategy

This is your Digital Marketing Mastery Playbook with the Power of One Marketing Concept. There are 15 fundamental building blocks in the playbook that can be applied to anything you want to sell.

Its simple yet powerful approach helps you understand your ideal customer and craft an offer they can't resist, leading to sales.

Please know this isn't a get-quick-results-in-30-days-and-under approach. Because there's no shortcut to success. Mastery requires clarity, discipline, practice, and a powerful mindset.

But before we start the process of building, understand some basics.

What is Integrated Digital Marketing?

"Integrated marketing communications is a way of looking at the whole marketing process from the viewpoint of the customer." — Philip Kotler

Integrated digital marketing is a strategic approach that combines multiple marketing channels, tactics, and tools to build a structure that meets business goals and delivers the best possible customer experience. The better your customer experience, the more sales you make.

Instead of operating in silos where each channel works independently, integrated digital marketing ensures all forms of digital and offline marketing communications are carefully aligned and interlinked.

What is Power of One Marketing?

The Power of One Marketing is a powerful approach in today's digital age, where customers expect brands to understand and cater to their unique preferences.

It has three key components:

1. One offer
2. One ideal customer
3. One clear call to action

Before you dive into the playbook, you must know your brand and your business goals for the current year and the next two to three years. The goals are very important because to get to where you want to be, you need to know where you want to go.

Your brand elements are business vision, mission, core values, your why, what you do, who you're serving, and how you're serving (your offers).

Let's Begin

1. Create one offer. Make sure the offer is:
   - Packed with value
   - Free or low-priced
   - Compelling enough to prompt a positive response

Example: ebook, subscription, demo, webinar, quiz, calculator, free discovery call

Once you have the email, you can drive people to other paid offers, upgrade to higher subscriptions, or sell a course—the opportunities are endless.

2. Write the summary of your offer and what it promises.
   - Summary:
   - Promise:

3. What is the expected outcome?
   - Get Email
   - Sell

4. Write down the call-to-action (CTA):
   - One CTA across all marketing tactics

Examples:
- Download Your Free Guide Now
- Learn From the Experts—Register Now
- Calculate Your Savings Now
- Explore Our Features—Get a Free Demo

5. Who is it for?

Think of one ideal customer and write everything you can imagine about them:

- What's the age, demographic, and income?
- What are the specific challenges they're looking to overcome?
- What is the benefit they're looking to achieve?
- What are their values, desires, and drives?
- What social media are they using?

Don't forget to consider all the touch points your customers will have with you post-purchase and make sure it's best-in-class. To me best-in-class means you strive for excellence in your work and your USP is so unique that your competitors can even touch it.

PRO TIP: The cost of new customer acquisition is way higher than the cost of retaining customers.

6. Write the USP (Unique Selling/Value Proposition).
   - How does your offer address their unique needs and challenges?
   - Keep it to three points.

7. Market Research:

   A. Analyze Competition
   - Write the three main competitors who are doing well with similar offers.
   - What marketing channels are they using to reach customers (organic and paid)?
   - What is their communication strategy? What is the CTA they are using?

   B. Consume and Experience
   - Follow content creators in related industries and consume their content.
   - Buy what they're selling to understand their sales funnel.
   - Attend events where you can talk to your audience.

   C. Personal Research
   - What form of content do you like to create?
   - What social media do you enjoy spending time on?
   - What makes you stop scrolling?

8. List all the ways you can get in front of your potential customers:

- This may include social media, networking, Eventbrite, trade shows, industry events, sponsorships, podcast appearances, speaking, workshops, etc.

PRO TIP: After listing all the ways, pick just one social media unless you have a team and a lot of time, then pick two.

9. Create your tactical plan:

The goal is to drive traffic to the landing page to get the customer to take the desired action.

PRO TIP:

- Pick the top three ways to get in front of the customer.
- Pick just one social media unless you have a team and a lot of time, then pick two.
- Create a robust email marketing plan (this is where magic happens). Remember, email marketing ROI is $42 per $1 you spend.

10. Create a funnel to generate leads:

Top of the Funnel: Woo the customer

- This is all about creating awareness, building trust, and establishing credibility.
- All the ways you can get in front of the customer (number 7) are top of the funnel.

Middle of the Funnel: Customer desires to learn more or engage

- Here, we aim to capture email addresses or sell a low-priced offer

- Landing page where the person you have been wooing may decide to engage with you

Bottom of the Funnel: Dating begins

- Customers like you enough to do business with you and basically pay for your services/products
- Email marketing, nurture existing customers, social media engagement, participation in workshops/masterminds/webinars

11. List the assets you'll need for execution:

Example: Landing page, Email CRM, Payment gateway, Scheduling link, Content strategy, Graphic software, Tools for video creation and editing, podcast.

12. Define the KPIs (Key Performance Indicators).

Your measure of success—it could include landing page visits, number of subscribers, certain revenue etc.

13. Write down why the customers should give you their time and money.

14. How you feel matters.

Are you feeling good about what you're selling? Do you believe in your offer? How do you feel about selling?

PRO TIP: If you're not comfortable selling and feel icky about it then no marketing plan will work effectively.

15. Execute the plan and revise as you learn more.

Make sure you review it once every six months. Continue to fine-tune it as you grow.

NOTE: Typically, it takes 8-12 hours of work to create a marketing strategy for your business.

Executing a successful digital marketing strategy requires clarity, discipline, and a relentless focus on delivering exceptional customer experiences.

By understanding your ideal customer, crafting irresistible offers, and leveraging integrated marketing tactics, you can create a seamless journey that builds trust and drives sales.

Remember, the journey of entrepreneurship is as much about mindset and resilience as it is about strategic execution. Trust your inner voice, embrace the learning from every experience, and keep pushing forward. Your dreams are within reach, and with the right strategy, you can turn them into reality.

Let this playbook guide you as you align your marketing efforts for customer success and build a thriving business that reflects your passion, purpose, and the impact you want to make in the life of others.

Prati Kaufman is a leading global marketing and human energy expert based in West Hartford, Connecticut. After 25+ years in marketing across the globe, working with everything from local entrepreneurs to Fortune 500+ corporations, she quit her job in 2019. Since then, she has grown from a one-person company to a full-service marketing agency. Her agency, Small Biz Marketing, helps small business owners get in front of the right audience with laser-focused, integrated marketing.

She is also a co-owner of a doggie daycare with her husband and plans to acquire more businesses in the next five years. She loves being an entrepreneur.

In her free time, you can find her hiking, camping, reading, and trying new food in different parts of the world.

Her biggest achievement so far has been raising a son who is totally in tune with himself and not afraid to be just him.

Connect with Prati:

Website: https://www.pratikaufman.com/
Instagram: https://www.instagram.com/pratikaufman/
LinkedIn: https://www.linkedin.com/in/pratikaufman/

Chapter 12

Networking That Doesn't Suck
How to Grow Your Influence with Key Partnerships
Donnie Boivin

> *Networking isn't about collecting contacts; it's about building relationships that matter. Cut the BS, get real, and watch your influence soar.*

My Story

As my networking skills grew, so did my business. But more importantly, I was building a legacy. I wasn't just known as a successful entrepreneur; I was seen as a connector, a leader, and someone who genuinely cared about helping others succeed.

One of the proudest moments of my career came when a young entrepreneur I had mentored for years told me how much my advice and support had meant to him. He said that by following the steps I taught him, he found his own way of selling that felt authentic and effective. He learned how to be a valuable asset to others, opening doors and creating opportunities for them. In the end, he built a company he could be proud of, one that reflected his values and vision.

This wasn't just about business; it was about making a real difference in someone's life. And that, my friends, is the true power of networking.

The Brutal Truth About My Networking Journey

I started out in the business world like most people—clueless and desperate for success. I wanted to win but didn't know how. I felt like I could be successful if I busted my ass, worked insane hours, and yet felt like I was getting nowhere. I believed hard work would get me to the top, but I was dead wrong.

The real game-changer? Networking.

My first venture was a disaster. I didn't know a damn thing about building connections. I thought attending a few networking events, handing out my business cards like candy, and making small talk would do the trick. Spoiler alert: it didn't. I was just another face in the crowd, blending in with all the other hopefuls who were equally clueless.

One day, I decided to stop playing it safe. I went to a local business event and made a conscious effort to genuinely engage. Instead of the mindless "Hi, I'm Donnie, here's my card," I focused on having real conversations. I approached strangers, introduced myself, and asked about their stories, looking for ways I could open doors for them. I discovered that asking how they got into their line of work sparked amazing dialogues.

That's when things started to change. People began to remember me, and more importantly, they started to trust me.

Learning the Hard Way

My initial approach to networking was about what I could get. I looked for quick wins and immediate returns, and frankly, it was a selfish strategy. It wasn't until I shifted my mindset to focus on building genuine relationships that I saw real results.

I met a guy named Mike at one of these events. He was running a marketing agency, and we clicked instantly. Instead of pitching my business right away, I asked, "So, how did you get into marketing?"

Mike smiled and started to share his story. "Well, it's a bit of a climb. I started out in the mailroom at a big agency. It wasn't glamorous, but I got to see how everything worked from the ground up. Over time, I worked my way up the ladder, learning everything I could about the industry."

"What made you decide to branch out on your own?" I asked, genuinely curious.

He leaned in, his eyes lighting up. "I realized that marketing is more than just pictures and words. It's about connecting with people on a human level. The big agency didn't see it that way. They were all about the numbers. I wanted to create campaigns that resonated with people, that told a story. So, I took the leap and started my own agency."

"That's inspiring," I said. "I know a couple of fantastic graphic designers and someone who specializes in promotional products. I think you'd really hit it off with them. Can I introduce you?"

Mike's eyes widened. "Absolutely, that would be amazing!"

I introduced Mike to my friends, Sarah and Tom, who were talented graphic designers, and Lisa, who was a whiz with promotional products. The introductions sparked immediate connections. Sarah and Tom were impressed by Mike's vision, and Lisa saw potential in collaborating on innovative marketing campaigns.

A few days later, Mike called me. "Hey, Donnie, I just wanted to thank you. Sarah, Tom, and Lisa are incredible. We're already brainstorming some exciting projects together."

"That's great to hear, Mike. I knew you guys would hit it off," I replied.

That small act of generosity led to a partnership that transformed my business. Mike and I began referring clients to each other, collaborating on projects, and soon enough, our businesses were thriving. One day, Mike called me with some exciting news.

"Donnie, I have to tell you something. We just landed a huge client, and it's all thanks to the team you helped me build. This is going to take both our businesses to the next level."

"Mike, that's incredible! I'm thrilled for you. It's amazing what can happen when we connect the right people."

Through this experience, I learned that networking is about more than just making contacts. It's about building relationships, offering value, and creating opportunities for others. And when you do that, the rewards come back to you tenfold.

The Strategy

How to Build Kick-Ass Partnerships

If you want to crush it in the networking game, you need a strategy. Here's the no-bullshit guide to building partnerships that will skyrocket your influence:

1. **Find Your Tribe:** Look for businesses that share your target audience but offer different services. These are your potential allies. You're not competing; you're complementing each other.

2. **Give Before You Take:** This is the golden rule. Offer something valuable before you ask for anything in return. Whether it's a referral, advice, or a connection—give first.

3. **Keep It Real:** Be honest about what you want and what you can offer. No one likes a shady dealer. Clear, open communication builds trust and sets the stage for a solid partnership.

4. **Stay Top of Mind:** Don't just show up once and disappear. Consistency is key. Regular check-ins, follow-ups, and genuine engagement keep the relationship alive.

5. **Leverage Online Tools:** Use social media and CRM systems to keep track of your connections and interactions. This helps you stay organized and ensures no relationship falls through the cracks.

One tool that has been a game-changer for me is my CRM system. It's not just about managing contacts; it's about tracking interactions, setting reminders, and making sure you're nurturing your relationships consistently. Think of it as your networking command center.

Creating a No-Bullshit Networking Plan

A killer networking plan is your roadmap to success. Here's how to create one that works:

1. **Define Your Goals:** Know exactly what you want to achieve. Is it more clients, better partners, or increased visibility? Get specific.

2. **Target the Right People:** Identify who can help you reach your goals. This means researching industries, companies, and individuals who align with your objectives.

3. **Do Your Homework:** Learn about your targets before you reach out. Understand their pain points, what they care about, and how you can help them.

4. **Make the First Move:** Don't wait for opportunities to come to you. Be proactive. Reach out with a clear, compelling message that shows you've done your homework.

5. **Follow Up Like a Pro:** The initial contact is just the beginning. Follow up with relevant information, invitations, or simply check in. This keeps the conversation going and builds the relationship.

6. **Evaluate and Adjust:** Regularly review your networking efforts. What's working? What's not? Adjust your strategy based on your results.

One of the most effective strategies I implemented was partnering with a local chamber of commerce. My goal was to become a well-known name in the community. I identified key players within the chamber and made it my mission to connect with them. I attended every event, volunteered for speaking engagements, and consistently provided value through resources and referrals. This not only expanded my network but also positioned me as a leader in my industry.

The Turning Point

As I continued to refine my networking strategy, I noticed a significant shift in how people responded to me. I was no longer just another business owner; I was a connector, a valuable resource, and someone people wanted to work with. This wasn't about luck; it was about intention and action.

One pivotal moment was when I decided to host my own networking events. I wanted to create a space where like-minded professionals could come together, share insights, and build meaningful relationships. These events weren't about sales pitches; they were about real conversations and genuine connections. The impact was immediate. People appreciated the authenticity, and my network grew exponentially.

Overcoming Challenges

Of course, it wasn't all smooth sailing. There were times when I felt like I was hitting a brick wall. Not every connection panned out, and not every effort yielded results. But I learned to see these setbacks as part of the process. Each failed attempt taught me something valuable about myself and my approach.

One of the toughest lessons was learning to let go of relationships that weren't serving me. It's easy to get caught up in the idea of having a vast network, but quality always trumps quantity. I began to focus on nurturing my most valuable connections and cutting ties with those who were draining my energy without offering any real benefit.

Advanced Tips for Building Rock-Solid Partnerships

1. **Identify Win-Win Opportunities:** Look for ways to create mutual benefit. This could be joint ventures, co-hosted events, or cross-promotional campaigns. The goal is to create value for both parties.

2. **Be a Connector:** Introduce your connections to each other. When you help others build their networks, you become a central, valuable node in the network.

3. **Invest in Relationships:** Spend time getting to know your key partners on a personal level. Relationships built on genuine connection are much stronger and more resilient.

4. **Show Appreciation:** A simple thank-you note or a small gesture of appreciation can go a long way. It shows that you value the relationship and are willing to invest in it.

5. **Stay Adaptable:** The business landscape is constantly changing. Be open to new opportunities and willing to pivot your strategy when necessary.

My CRM system plays a crucial role in managing these advanced strategies. By keeping detailed notes on each interaction, setting follow-up reminders, and tracking the progress of my partnerships, I ensure that no opportunity is missed and no relationship is neglected.

Crafting a Strategic Networking Plan That Delivers

Let's break down the steps of creating a killer networking plan:

1. **Set Clear, Actionable Goals:** What do you want to achieve? More clients? Strategic partnerships? Increased industry influence? Be specific and set measurable objectives.

2. **Identify Your Ideal Connections:** Who can help you reach these goals? Create a list of target industries, companies, and key individuals.

3. **Research Thoroughly:** Know everything you can about your targets. What are their pain points? How can you provide value? This knowledge will set you apart from the rest.

4. **Craft a Compelling Outreach Message:** Your first impression matters. Craft a message that is personal, relevant, and demonstrates that you've done your homework.

5. **Be Proactive and Persistent:** Don't wait for opportunities to come to you. Reach out, follow up, and stay engaged. Persistence is often the key to breaking through.

6. **Regularly Review and Adjust Your Plan:** What's working? What's not? Regularly review your efforts and adjust your strategy based on what you learn.

One of the most successful applications of this strategy was my engagement with a national association in my industry. My goal was to become a recognized authority within this network. I started by identifying key members and influencers. I researched their challenges and provided valuable insights through blog posts, webinars, and one-on-one meetings. Over time, I built strong relationships with several key figures, leading to speaking engagements, collaborations, and a significant boost in my industry reputation.

Leveraging Technology for Maximum Impact

In today's digital age, leveraging technology is essential for effective networking. Here are some advanced tips:

1. **Utilize Social Media Strategically:** Platforms like LinkedIn, Twitter, and even Instagram can be powerful tools for building and nurturing your network. Share valuable content, engage with your connections' posts, and participate in relevant groups and discussions.

2. **Implement a CRM System:** A good CRM system is invaluable for managing your network. Track your interactions, set follow-up reminders, and keep detailed notes on each contact. This ensures that no relationship is overlooked.

3. **Host Virtual Events:** With the rise of remote work, virtual events have become a powerful way to connect with your network. Webinars, virtual coffee chats, and online workshops can help you stay engaged with your connections, no matter where they are.

4. **Automate Where Possible:** Use tools like email automation and social media scheduling to streamline your networking efforts. This frees up time to focus on building genuine connections.

5. **Analyze and Optimize:** Regularly review your networking activities and analyze the results. Use this data to optimize your strategy and ensure you're focusing your efforts where they'll have the most impact.

Real-World Application of Strategic Networking

Putting your networking strategy into action requires a combination of planning, execution, and adaptability. Here's how to make it happen:

1. **Identify Key Events and Opportunities:** Look for industry conferences, networking events, and online forums where your target connections are likely to be. Plan your participation and set specific goals for each event.

2. **Prepare Your Pitch:** Whether you're introducing yourself in person or online, have a clear, concise pitch that communicates who you are, what you do, and how you can provide value. Practice until it feels natural.

3. **Engage Authentically:** At events, focus on building genuine connections rather than collecting business cards. Ask questions, listen actively, and look for opportunities to help.

4. **Follow Up Diligently:** After an event, follow up with your new connections promptly. Reference your conversation, offer additional value, and propose a next step, such as a coffee meeting or a call.

5. **Maintain and Nurture Relationships:** Use your CRM system to track follow-ups and set reminders for regular check-ins.

Share relevant content, offer support, and stay engaged to keep your relationships strong.

6. **Evaluate and Adjust:** After each event or networking initiative, review your results. What went well? What could be improved? Use this feedback to refine your approach for next time.

One of my most successful real-world applications of strategic networking was at an industry conference. I went in with a clear plan: I researched the attendees, identified key individuals I wanted to connect with, and prepared my pitch. Throughout the conference, I focused on building genuine connections, asking insightful questions, and offering value. After the event, I followed up with each contact, referencing our conversations and proposing the next steps. This approach led to several valuable partnerships and significantly expanded my network.

By following the principles and strategies outlined in this mini-book, you can revolutionize your approach to networking, build powerful partnerships, and grow your influence like never before. Real networking is about cutting through the noise, being genuine, and creating value for everyone involved. Start today, and watch your network become your greatest asset.

If you sell business-to-business and are tired of networking with people who sell business-to-consumer, come visit one of our Success Champion Networking groups. We've redefined B2B networking to create the connections you've always wanted. Join us and experience how networking should be done. Go to https://successchampionnetworking.com

Donnie Boivin is an unapologetic, no-BS entrepreneur, speaker, and author dedicated to teaching professionals how to master the art of networking. With over two decades of experience in the business world, Donnie has transformed countless lives and businesses through his raw, real approach to building meaningful relationships. He is the founder of Success Champion Networking, a community that fosters growth through collaboration and support. Donnie's mission is to empower others to unlock their potential and achieve extraordinary success through strategic networking.

Connect with Donnie:

LinkedIn: https://www.linkedin.com/in/donnieboivin/

Success Champion Networking: https://successchampionnetworking.com

Chapter 13

Podcasting

The Easy Way to Empowerment, Growth, and Success

S.A. Grant, Founder and Host of Boss Uncaged

> *Life is parallel to existence but perpendicular to time. Seize the opportunity for empowerment, growth, and success at every intersection.*

My Story

It was a beautiful autumn evening, and I was driving to my future wife's apartment. I parked at the parking deck and headed into the building, passing through the gym as usual. However, something felt different. Walking, I suddenly felt a burning sensation and started sweating profusely. I decided to take a cold shower in the gym with my clothes on to cool down, but unfortunately, it didn't help, nor does it make much sense looking back.

I abruptly felt unwell and struggled to get from the first to the fourth floor. I suddenly fell to the floor. *Am I just overheated?*

I managed to gather enough strength to get back on my feet with the help of a door handle. Strangely, my right foot felt numb, almost like it had fallen asleep.

I found myself in a zombie-like state, pressed against the wall and slowly inching forward, dragging half of my body along. I could've easily been cast for *The Walking Dead*. I transitioned into the elevator, but to this day, still can't remember how or when I even pressed the buttons.

Mentally, I laugh about the jokes I used to make about her super-long hallway leading from her elevator to her apartment - easily 100+ yards - but at that moment, it might as well have been the Boston Marathon.

As time passed, seconds felt like minutes, and minutes felt like hours. I was relieved as I approached the door. I was utterly exhausted, wet, sweating, and boiling, but I made it. The only thing left was to use the keys and unlock the door. *You can do it. Just get the key into the lock!* However, this simple task felt like the creepy scratching on a door you experience in horror movies. For the life of me, I couldn't control my arm as it flew all over the door in an attempt to get the key in the damn lock.

I heard the cylinder on the lock turn. The door slowly cracked open, and I collapsed in her arms. I pushed into the bathroom and immediately reached for more cold water. She looked puzzled, concerned, and bewildered. I faintly remember hearing her voice ask, "What's going on? Are you okay?"

In a sudden moment of reality, the air sucked out of the room. I tried to speak, but nothing came out of my mouth. Thoughts raced through my mind. *Damn, there is a glitch in my code! Am I going to have to learn sign language? How long will this last?* I hunched over the bathtub, clutching the cold water.

"OMG! I'm calling the ambulance," she shrieked. With immense effort, I managed to mumble out one word: "No!" I saw the fear in her eyes as we locked gazes for the first time that night. She immediately understood what was happening. Time seemed to accelerate, rushing past us.

What seemed like milliseconds later, the EMTs burst into the bathroom, looking at me in amazement as I paced without the ability to speak. They strapped me to the gurney and put me in the ambulance. Then, suddenly, almost instantly, everything went black—a complete void that seemed infinite, with sporadic noise and bursts of light. My eyes slowly crept open.

Holy shit, it's a halo; This is what I've heard about in the movies. Am I dead? I still find this moment funny, as the halo was the surgery lights. Almost on cue, I hear a single beep, and then I'm sucked back into the void. In the void, there is no essence of time. It could've been an eternity. But suddenly, I woke up in a hospital bed, confused about what had happened exactly. I looked over and saw my family in the room, looking at me with relief. I scratched my inner thigh, and to my surprise, there was a massive bandage on my leg.

"WTF happened?"

"You had a stroke!" someone yelled out.

I paused for a minute. When I heard "The silent killer," I nodded and said, "Wow, that's interesting. A stroke? Hmm."

"Okay, so how long before we check out today?" Once the doctors entered and I was presented with my first meal, I was confronted with the bewildering realization of what had happened.

The following is from my medical report, so don't be alarmed if it doesn't make sense, considering it's primarily written in medical jargon.

On 10/14/2018 at 10:37 pm, Abnormal CT perfusion of the brain in the distribution of the left middle cerebral artery with a small core infarct and large surrounding penumbra.

The Medical Narrative

HISTORY: Aphasia, right facial droop.

Technique: *Following the IV administration of 40 ccs of Isovue-370 nonionic contrast, whole-brain helical CT perfusion was performed on a 256-slice CT scanner. Following the acquisition of the source data set, the study was post-processed, and CBV, CBF,*

MTT and Tmax maps were generated using RAPID post-processing software. Low-dose radiation techniques were used.

Findings: *There is a small region of abnormal CBV and CBF in the distribution of the left middle cerebral artery, with a larger area of abnormally prolonged MTT and Tmax, suggesting a core infarct with surrounding penumbra.*

Core Infarct (CBF <30%): 29 cc's.

Tmax >6 sec: 145 cc's

Mismatch: 116 cc's"

The translation: Think of it like my brain is having a rough day, and the doctors are using their sci-fi gadgets to figure out what's happening. I was fortunate but wholly fucked up sums it up!

As I continued listening to the odds, I started eating. I began to see how exactly I was screwed. The right side of my body's motor functions were drastically reduced to a falling (flailing?) beached fish. I was barely able to hold the spoon and completely missed my mouth. *This is going to be interesting.*

"Alright, doctor, so what's the plan? How can I get out of here as soon as possible?"

"You need to be able to stand up and walk completely independently, eat independently, and function independently."

"Got it; it's time to make it happen."

Seconds after the doctor left the room, I immediately tried to stand up and start walking. The alarm went off; my nurse rushed into my room. "Are you okay?"

"Yes! The doctor said that for me to get out of the hospital, I had to walk on my own. Don't worry. I got my boss-wife by my side; we got this; there's no need to worry. So, let's get going, bebe." The nurse had this look like "Since you put it that way, go and get it, sir."

What does this life-changing depiction of a near-death experience have to do with *Podcasting: The Easy Way to Empowerment, Growth, & Success?*

Growth and success don't happen overnight. First, it took me a few days to achieve what the doctor asked, and that Friday, I checked out of the hospital.

During that time, my future wife and I had a life-changing conversation. I initially developed a passion for graffiti in Brooklyn during the 90s. This led to my pursuing a career as a graphic designer and later transitioning to web designer and multimedia expert in the early 2000s. While working as an IT professional at a local art college, I discovered a love for video and audio. Over the next few years, I explored various job roles, seeking fulfillment and gaining experience. Along the way, I held titles such as Web Designer, Creative Director, and IT Director, to name a few.

I've always had a strong desire to become an entrepreneur. Like many of you seeking answers, I tried my hand at various ventures. I transformed my freelance graphic design and web design business into a corporation, Serebral Media Inc. I focused on acquiring clients needing branding, marketing, web development, and consulting services. Not stopping there, I delved into multi-level marketing and the financial sector and obtained licenses in Life Insurance, Property and Casualty, and Series 6. I built financial teams across different states, from New York to Atlanta. As if that wasn't enough, I also ventured into the travel industry and became a travel agent. And to top it off, I became a first-time author. Looking back, it seems amusing how I racked up accomplishments like kids collecting new social media accounts.

I managed all of these responsibilities while being a full-time single dad. Our daily routine involved:

- Waking up.
- Getting my son ready for school.
- Taking him to school.
- Managing my businesses.
- Attending client meetings.
- Address any urgent issues until I pick him up.

After school, I took him to extracurricular activities and sometimes coached his basketball and flag football teams. Additionally, I was involved in various school-related activities, such as being a Cub Scout assistant den leader, PTA president, and the Creative Director of the school's foundation. In the evenings, I participated in conference calls and meetings, made dinner, brainstormed new ideas, and worked on action plans for more licenses, all while ensuring my son was taken care of. Finally, I'd put him to bed, catch up on reading, and take action on any new knowledge I acquired.

Step and repeat until the cumulative effect of long hours, stress, and genetics led to my stroke.

My future wife locked eyes with me and uttered words that shaped our future: "What are you going to do now? You have been forced to hit the reset button. Why don't you take this as the opportunity to rebrand yourself as you have worked and helped many companies before? It's time for you to step into the limelight."

At that moment, she became my inspiration, superwoman, and everything. I felt a furious energy of supernatural origin surge through me and ignite a fire I never felt before. I then searched for the means to help me achieve this rebranding exploration.

I felt a surge of excitement, but then reality struck hard. The upcoming months in my recovery journey would be incredibly challenging. It felt like stretching the fabric of my silver lining was the most formidable challenge I ever faced. From making adjustments like speaking slower (which is painful for a native New Yorker) to grappling with the frustration of my mind racing while my mouth lagged, it was like watching a movie on dial-up with constant buffering.

My once firm grip weakened, leaving me powerless, like a passionate rock climber unable to do a single pull-up. There were moments when my laser-like focus on tasks waned, leaving me feeling like a car struggling to start in the depths of winter. I felt like so much of who I was had vanished, and I experienced true depression for the first time. It was a darkness far more insidious than I could've imagined, and I understand now why some people succumb to its grasp. Although I never admitted it then, thoughts of ending it all crossed my mind. Yet, I refused to surrender. Despite depression's relentless grip, I fought back fiercely, refusing to let it thwart my destiny. Gradually, slivers of my former self emerged. As my focus returned, I started exploring next steps and options for stepping into the limelight.

After considering different options, such as becoming an online drop shipper, a YouTuber, an author, and an online day trader, I searched through networking outlets, summits, and events to find a source of inspiration. Four hundred sixty-five days later, on January 22, 2020, at 6:30 pm EST, I had a breakthrough.

I attended a gathering at a podcast recording studio, and it was filled with like-minded podcasters. I couldn't believe it—I found my tribe and the industry I could grow into, and that would support my rebranding efforts. This discovery happened just 15 months after I had a stroke and made a full recovery.

Not only did I find the path to my rebranding, but I also found my calling. Less than 30 days later, I rebranded myself as S.A. Grant and became the Founder and host of The Boss Uncaged Podcast. This was the beginning of a new chapter for me.

Podcasting could be the new beginning that helps you discover what you've been seeking.

The Strategy

My journey from a stroke survivor to a successful podcast host is a testament to the transformative power of podcasting. It empowered me, spurred my growth, and catalyzed my success. This strategy guide will help you leverage podcasting to achieve your empowerment, development, and success.

1. Discover Your Why—Purpose and Passion

Identify Your Core Message: What story do you want to tell? What expertise or insights do you have that can inspire or educate others?

Define Your Audience: Who will benefit most from your content? Knowing your target audience will help tailor your content to meet their needs and interests.

My Example: The Boss Uncaged Podcast

Core Message: Sharing stories of resilience, entrepreneurship, and growth.

Target Audience: Aspiring entrepreneurs, business owners, and individuals seeking personal development.

2. Plan Your Content—Content Strategy

Themes and Topics: Choose themes that align with your core message and are relevant to your audience.

Episode Format: Decide on a format that suits your style and content—interviews, solo episodes, or panel discussions.

Frequency and Consistency: Determine a realistic schedule for releasing episodes. Consistency is critical to building an audience.

My Example: Content Planning

Themes: Resilience, entrepreneurship, digital marketing, personal development.

Format: Interviews with successful entrepreneurs and solo episodes sharing personal insights.

Schedule: Weekly episodes are released every Tuesday at 5 a.m. EST.

3. Set Up Your Podcast—Technical Setup

Equipment: Invest in a good microphone, headphones, and recording software. Ensure a quiet recording environment.

Hosting Platform: Choose a reliable podcast hosting platform to upload and distribute your episodes.

My Example: Technical Setup

Equipment: High-quality microphone, soundproofing, and editing software.

Hosting Platform: Bcast for easy distribution across significant podcast directories.

4. Launch and Promote—Launch Strategy

Pre-Launch Hype: Create anticipation with teasers and sneak peeks.

Launch Day: Release multiple episodes on the launch day to give new listeners substantial content to enjoy.

Promotion

Social Media: Leverage social media platforms to promote episodes.

Guest Promotion: Encourage guests to share episodes with their network.

Email Marketing: Build an email list and send regular updates to subscribers.

My Example: Launch and Promotion

Pre-Launch: Teasers and behind-the-scenes content on social media.

Launch Day: Released three episodes to kickstart the podcast.

Promotion: Consistent social media updates, guest promotions, and email newsletters.

5. **Engage and Grow Your Audience—Audience Engagement**

Listener Interaction: Encourage listeners to send feedback, ask questions, and suggest topics.

Community Building: Create a community around your podcast through social media groups or forums.

Growth Strategies

Collaborations: Partner with other podcasters and influencers.

SEO: Optimize your podcast titles and descriptions for search engines.

Analytics: Use analytics to track performance and refine your strategy.

My Example: Engagement and Growth

Listener Interaction: Regular Q&A segments and listener shout-outs.

Community: A dedicated Facebook group for listeners.

Collaborations: Guest appearances on other podcasts.

6. **Monetize Your Podcast—Monetizing Podcasts Shortlist Options**

Sponsorships: Partner with brands that align with your podcast's theme.

Merchandise: Sell branded merchandise to your audience.

Memberships: Offer premium content or early access through a membership model.

My Example: Monetization

Sponsorships: Partnered with relevant brands for sponsorship deals.

Merchandise: Launched a line of branded merchandise.

Memberships: Exclusive education content on the Boss Uncaged Academy for subscribers.

Conclusion

Podcasting can empower, inspire growth, and pave the way to success. Following this strategy, you can build a podcast that resonates with your audience and fulfills your personal and professional goals. The key to successful podcasting lies in your passion, consistency, and engagement with your listeners. If I rose from the ashes of a stroke to build a thriving podcast, you can conquer your epic journey and embark on your empowerment, growth, and success with podcasting. Welcome to the ride of a lifetime, Boss.

S. A. Grant is the driving force behind Boss Uncaged Omnimedia Inc. He is the Founder and Host of the Boss Uncaged Podcast, where he shares his expertise in digital marketing, branding, and business growth strategy. With 25 years of experience dedicated to helping businesses, S. A. Grant has become a prominent figure in the industry.

His journey began in Brooklyn, where his passion for graffiti art ignited a lifelong love for creativity. After graduating from The Art Institute of Atlanta with degrees in Graphic Design, Web Design, and Multimedia, he started a career as a Digital Marketing, Brand, and Growth Strategy Consultant.

Grant is known for delivering results. He is a #1 best-selling author, and his notebook series is a valuable resource for aspiring entrepreneurs. His company, Boss Uncaged Omnimedia Inc., is dedicated to creating innovative business strategies and tactics.

In addition to consulting, Grant has been a guest on numerous international podcasts and a sought-after speaker at prestigious events. He finds joy in coaching and mentoring authors, podcasters, entrepreneurs, educators, and publishers, helping them create content, develop automation, and repurpose existing content effectively.

S. A. Grant's dedication to empowerment, growth, and success is evident in every aspect of his career. His journey from a passionate artist in Brooklyn to a leading figure in digital marketing and business strategy is a testament to his relentless drive, creativity, and commitment to excellence.

S. A. Grant enjoys global travel, rock climbing, sailing, mixed martial arts, impromptu chess games, food tours, and spending quality time with his family. In 2024, he and his family relocated to Amsterdam, Netherlands, embracing their adventurous spirit.

Connect with S.A.:

Website: https://bossuncaged.com/

Podcast: https://podcast.bossuncaged.com/

Contact: https://qr.io/r/OmNZ8l

Follow S.A. on Social Media

https://qr.io/r/1GSfBH

S. A. Bonus Quick Links: https://qr.io/r/XkOZga

Chapter 14

Dare to Be Different
"Your Way" May Be the Best Way!
Dr. Ahriana Platten

> *If I could teach the world just one thing, it would be that choice is your superpower. It charts the course for your entire life. Good choices make your dreams come true!*

My Story

My father taught me three invaluable lessons about life and business:

1. "If someone asks you to do something you've never done, and you believe you can do it, say yes."

2. "You can do anything you want to do -- if you're willing to work hard enough at it."

3. "Despite others opinions, you'll often find your way is the best way. Trust your gut."

These guiding principles shaped my professional life and continue to steer me toward uncharted territories. I'm hoping these words will give you the confidence you need to do things your way, because I believe your way—and being exactly who you are—is why you're here on planet Earth.

It took a long time for me to learn this. After a foreign exchange trip to Brazil, I got married too young, had two children, and divorced before our second anniversary because I was being physically abused. Despite bruises and heart-wrenching rejection, I'd come to believe it was me who failed at marriage rather than my abuser, and that left me wondering how I could possibly succeed at parenting.

I didn't sign up to do this alone! I love these kids with my whole heart, but how am I going to support them?

I needed a job that accommodated my parenting responsibilities, and I needed it quick! I applied for a position teaching K-8 music and art at a private school that didn't require a teaching license. *It's just singing and drawing, right?!* This was my first foray into "doing it my way." The school offered no training, only a few supplies, and a classroom that filled and emptied several times a day with kids ranging from five to fourteen. The learning curve was incredibly steep, and I stumbled often. Believe me, no one was more surprised that I succeeded than I was! I loved working with the kids, and we had tons of fun together. And, for a while, that was enough.

However, as time passed, I kept revisiting the idea of becoming a broadcaster. It was a lifetime dream. Knowing I'd need help to make it happen, I packed up my children and moved to another state where I could live with my parents. I bravely applied for a reporting position at a radio station despite having no experience. Remarkably, they hired me.

"You're a great speaker! Just be you! This button turns the mic on, and this one turns it off."

Oh my God! Are you kidding? That's my training?

Jumping in with both feet, I learned to write and read the news, choose and play music, and fill out reports—all by trial and error. I interviewed people and took a lot of deep breaths as I mustered the courage to ask questions other people might have felt were too controversial. Within months, my candor got me a job offer for an airborne traffic reporter position, flying twice daily over two major cities in a small two-seater Cessna aircraft, serving twenty-six radio stations.

"Do you like to fly in small planes?" the producer asked. "I love it!" I responded.

I had never flown in a small plane.

Before I knew it, I was 1500 feet in the air, face pressed against the window of the plane as it circled a five-car pile-up. My stomach churned as we flew around and around, and I thought I was going to throw up. But I didn't. I swallowed my fear, along with whatever threatened to exit my body, and pushed the "click-to-talk" button to give my report. "Better find a different way home, friends. This one is going to take a long time to clear. Traffic is already backed up as far as I can see." Sheer stubbornness got me (and my grumpy tummy) through the initial days. I had a blast bantering with the disc jockeys and was certain I'd found the career I'd be in for the rest of my life.

I was wrong about that.

My broadcast career ended abruptly eight years later when I went to a client meeting with a radio station manager. On the way, he told me a secret. "We don't really run all the advertising this company pays for. How would they know? They certainly don't sit around all day counting commercials!"

My conscience got the best of me, and a few days later, I met with the client and told them what had been said. I knew I'd be fired, and I was, but I had a new idea! I opened an advertising agency with that advertiser as my first client, and believe me, we counted commercials!

The following summer, while manning a booth for my agency at a marketing convention, I was offered a job by the chairman of a London-based development company. He needed someone to lead a research team and write market feasibility studies—something I'd never done before.

"You should get out and see the world! I think you'd be a great addition to my team. Why don't you come to work for me?"

Is this guy serious? How could I possibly travel the world with kids at home? But what if he's actually serious? This could be a once-in-a-lifetime opportunity!

"I'd be very interested! I'm not sure if I can make it work, but I'd love to try," I replied.

Together, we found a way to make it work, formed a partnership, and for twenty-one years, I traveled, leading teams across different countries and placing my feet (and heart) on different continents. From Mexico to Mongolia and Vietnam to Hungary, I shared meals with millionaires and beggars alike, learning from every situation I encountered.

I was in my forties when I started my seminary training, and I was fifty-two when I received my Ph.D.

Why This Matters for You

It's simple: I want you to notice that I never did a single thing in the "normal" way. Not. One. Thing.

There is no "one way" or "right way" to do anything. There's your way and someone else's way. You only become an expert when you learn how to do things your way. Formal education is invaluable, but it only takes you so far. The path to mastery is built one step at a time, one experience at a time—and it takes courage. My unconventional journey gave me the expertise that develops through risk-taking, asking good questions, and trying new things.

If I can do it, so can you.

There's a Transformational Aspect: Teaching

Business and spirituality intersect in my life, and nothing I write would be complete without mentioning the transformative nature of your entrepreneurial adventure. It doesn't matter whether you follow a specific religious path, consider yourself 'spiritual but not religious,' or are more humanist, and don't subscribe to any spiritual practice. What matters is that life itself is holy, and all of us can make the world better if we choose to.

At some point on our journey, many of us are given the opportunity to become teachers. Transitioning from learning a skill to becoming an expert and then moving on to teach others often involves a soul-journey that benefits you and the world at large. As we deepen our knowledge and refine our skills, we become conduits for wisdom and inspiration. Sharing our hard-earned insights enriches the collective consciousness, fostering a more enlightened and compassionate society. My unusual set of life skills was ultimately the result of a willingness to use imagination and innovation to problem solve. Teaching others what I learned along the way seemed to be the natural next step. That may also be true for you.

In many spiritual traditions, being given the role of the teacher is the outcome of overcoming challenges. I certainly had more than a few of those in my life. A master teacher doesn't just impart knowledge but also nurtures the spirit of the learner, offering compassion and helping them realize their potential. This sacred exchange transforms both the teacher and the student.

Embracing this role requires humility, openness, and a deep sense of responsibility. It's about recognizing that our journey isn't just for our personal growth but also for the greater good. By sharing our stories, challenges, and triumphs, we offer others the courage to embark on their own journeys with confidence and hope.

The Strategy

So, how does one step into teaching? This, my friends, is another character-building opportunity! First, you must be willing to recognize that you have something important to share—and then make yourself available to authentically share it.

Teaching is how we pass on our wisdom, and it's also a strategic business move that can significantly impact your business growth, brand authority, and revenue streams. Not everyone is suited for teaching, but if you are, you'll be surprised how many people are eager to access your knowledge and, more importantly, your unique perspective. And teaching is a whole new learning path for you personally. The process of converting what you've learned into a language other people can understand will deepen and clarify what your professional journey has taught you.

The Rising Demand for Online Learning

There are many ways to teach: Speaking in person, through written formats such as blogs and books, and on digital platforms. Although I do a lot of public speaking, I'm most fond of digital teaching, live on Zoom, or through pre-recorded programs people can watch at their convenience. When I teach online, my students come from around the world. I love that so much! It keeps me growing my international clientele, and I can do it from anywhere I travel.

In case you wonder if there's money to be made, consider a recent report by Global Market Insights. In this report, the e-learning market is projected to exceed $375 billion by 2026. That's because e-learning offers many benefits. Learners can access courses anytime, anywhere, which is ideal for busy professionals, and online courses often cost less than traditional education, providing an affordable alternative for your clients.

Diversifying Revenue Streams

Income is important for all of us. I love making money – especially when I can make it in my sleep! Online courses can generate passive income with minimal costs, which translates to higher profit margins. Some experts offer courses through a subscription model, ensuring recurring revenue. Others place their courses on digital platforms that handle marketing for them. And, naturally, courses serve as a gateway to introduce people to other products or services you offer.

Enhancing Customer Loyalty and Engagement

Another benefit of teaching is that courses can significantly enhance your customer's loyalty and engagement. Providing educational content adds value to the customer experience, fostering appreciation and loyalty, and interactive elements like forums and live Q&A sessions create a sense of community and more meaningful relationships with those you serve.

Leveraging Data and Analytics

Oh, the things you can track online! Creating online courses provides valuable data and analytics that can inform broader business strategies. Tracking completion rates, feedback, and engagement levels help refine offerings and improve quality. Analyzing course content can highlight trends and inform product development and marketing strategies. These insights enable data-driven decisions, enhancing overall effectiveness.

Building Partnerships and Networks

One more thing: course creation opens doors for strategic partnerships and network building. Partnering with industry experts or businesses to co-create courses can expand reach and credibility. Collaboration replaces competition as our most effective path to success.

Implementing affiliate programs can drive traffic and sales, leverage other people's networks, and build awareness of your offerings. Most affiliate programs offer revenue when your recommendation generates a product sale.

And, offering tailored courses and employee training for other companies can establish lucrative B2B (Business-to-Business) relationships and expand the reach of your unique teachings, opening even more pathways to success.

It's Time to Step Up to the Challenge

From establishing expertise and diversifying revenue streams to enhancing customer loyalty and leveraging data, the benefits of teaching are substantial. Maybe it's time to ask yourself if you're ready to teach others what you've learned.

Before You Record, Ask What They Want

I started offering online courses in 2018. At the time, "evergreen" courses (pre-recorded with a long shelf life) were trending. Today, evergreen is still very popular, and learners prefer shorter courses to longer ones. I find people are more willing to purchase a course with three twenty-minute classes over a forty-five to sixty-minute full-length course. This allows people to break up their learning experience into small, bite-sized pieces that meet their time or attention limits.

A word of hard-earned advice: Your clients know what they want to learn. Spend a little time talking with them before creating courses. You might be surprised by their needs. I thought my clients wanted a comprehensive course on world religions, but they preferred short, practical guidance on things like building home altars and how to move through grief and loss.

Also, consider offering a weekly Q&A for course purchasers. Doing a live Q&A connects you with people interested in your work and often translates into paying clients who want personal support.

The Power of Sharing Wisdom

Becoming a master teacher is your gift to the world. As you delve deeper into your field and offer your expertise, it's essential to remember the impact that comes from sharing what you've learned. Each of us has unique wisdom to share, shaped by our experiences, challenges, and triumphs. When we share our insights authentically, we contribute to a collective pool of knowledge that benefits others and shifts consciousness. It's valuable to consider that wisdom is gained not only through our successes but also through our ability to overcome the harder moments of life.

Don't be afraid to share a bit about the more challenging aspects of your work. My friend Connie would say, "Don't bleed all over everyone!" It's not necessary to share every gory detail. But allowing some insight into how you handle challenges or failures will help others feel they, too, can overcome unexpected hurdles and find their path to purpose-driven success.

Trust that the people who need your unique talents will find their way to you if you make yourself visible. The power of the whole universe is behind you as you share your wisdom with those who need it.

The Advice I Give to Everyone

If I could teach the world just one thing, it would be that choice is your superpower. It charts the course for your entire life. Good choices make your dreams come true! And if you're looking for a mentor to support you in being who you truly are, I am as close as the contact information below:

Rev. Dr. Ahriana Platten is a priestess, pastor, and peacemaker. As a master ceremonialist, spiritual educator, and business guide, she offers the tools necessary to transform your life. With more than thirty-five years of experience, Ahriana has touched the hearts of thousands of people around the world and influenced great change. She's a global wisdom keeper, a soul-shifting mentor, and an inspired speaker who weaves together purpose-driven business and sacred spirituality to support those who desire to make everything they touch better than they found it.

Ahriana is the best-selling author of *Rites and Rituals, Harnessing the Power of Sacred Ceremony* and *The Changing Story*, an award-winning children's book. She's a former Ambassador for the Parliament of the World's Religions and has traveled across five continents (so far), visiting 16 different countries. She's addressed elders and spiritual leaders from over 250 tribes and traditions and is a featured spiritual teacher in the docuseries *Time of the Sixth Sun*.

In addition to sharing her wisdom through her global online community, *ASoulfulWorld.com*, Ahriana travels the world with her soulmate, a wild and deep-hearted man, and is mother to five incredibly creative adults. Ahriana's spare time is spent enjoying good coffee at street-side cafes, taking photos of whatever beautiful thing catches her eye, and sharing new experiences with her ever-curious grandchildren.

Connect with Ahriana:

Website: https://www.asoulfullworld.com
Receive a free gift at https://www.asoulfullworld.com/simpleceremonies

Instagram: https://www.instagram.com/ahriana_platten/

Facebook: https://www.facebook.com/profile.php?id=61555187993178

LinkedIn: https://www.linkedin.com/in/ahriana-platten-b4170613/

Schedule a free thirty-minute "get-to-know-each-other" call at https://www.asoulfullworld.com/activate

Chapter 15

A Business *V*isual *M*asterpiece
Graphic Design that Establishes Identity and Sells
Tanya Stokes

> *Creating unique graphic designs is the key to distinguishing your brand and driving sales to new heights.*

My Story

"Fuck it! I quit!"

For over 20 years, I chased the elusive dream of working in the graphic design industry. It felt as though the universe shouted a resounding "Hell no!" at me. I longed to be surrounded by top-tier talent, hoping their knowledge and expertise would guide me to success. But every time a door seemed to crack open, it slammed shut just as quickly.

Frustrated, I turned to my side hustles, branding myself as a Creative Specialist. This included painting murals—yes, painting on walls, the kind of painting that got me in trouble as a child. Photography was another passion.

Oh, how I love a great candid shot, capturing people being their natural selves. That creative flow that translates into a masterpiece is what gets my engine going. I was fed up with not having enough time to immerse myself in my passion—design. It was my therapy, my sanctuary, and lately, I needed it more than ever.

Juggling the demands of being a single mom of three with a "good government job" that provided stability was overwhelming. While I was grateful for the security, I couldn't envision myself there forever. I yearned for more. I watched my coworkers labor and retire, only to scramble to fulfill their dreams in their late 50s or, tragically, pass away before achieving their desires. I refused to become that person.

Yet, I was plagued by self-doubt.

I'm not good enough to quit my job.

There are so many designers better than me. No one will hire me without the experience they have.

One day, lost in these thoughts, I scrolled through Facebook. I saw people living their lives freely, exploring the world, doing what they loved whenever they wanted. Envy gnawed at me. Just when I thought I was at my breaking point, a notification appeared—a message in my inbox.

It was from the renowned Laura Di Franco! Laura Di Franco is a true powerhouse in the publishing industry, known not only for her incredible mentorship but also for her remarkable track record of over 70 Amazon #1 bestsellers. If you haven't heard of her, you should definitely look her up—her influence and success are nothing short of inspiring.

My heart raced as I stared at the message. Why is she reaching out to me? A whirlwind of excitement, doubt, and concern surged through my mind, creating a storm of emotions. It feels now, as I type, as vivid and surreal as if it had happened yesterday.

The message arrived around 8 am:

"Would you be interested in helping me with the cover design for the poetry collab?"

I stared at that message all day long, unable to tear my eyes away from the screen. Breakfast, lunch, and dinner came and went in a blur as I repeatedly checked my inbox to make sure it was real. I didn't tell anyone. Normally, I'd consult a friend about my next business move, but this time, I chose to reflect on my past work alone. I thought about the book covers I designed—*My Muse, The Truth, The Butterfly Effect, The Girl with the Iron Leg, Because She Had Something to Say*, and many others. I remembered the satisfaction and pride in the authors' eyes when they saw the final results—always pleased with the outcome.

After 12 hours of intense reflection and self-doubt, I finally summoned the courage to reply to Laura. Imposter syndrome hit hard. *Can I do this? Writing poetry was one thing, but creating a book cover for someone I secretly admired was a different story altogether. What are her expectations going to be? Why did she choose me?*

These endless narratives swirled with no conclusions, each one adding to the pressure building inside. Every thought and memory demanded attention, pulling me in different directions. The excitement of the opportunity, the fear of falling short, and the curiosity about Laura's intentions all mingled together, creating a cacophony of emotions.

I knew this was a pivotal moment in my career, one that could define my future in ways I couldn't yet imagine. And so, with trembling fingers and a heart full of hope and fear, I typed my response and hit send, stepping into the unknown.

My response at 8:45 pm:

"It would be an honor!"

We set up a date to meet, and *BAM!* we dove right into her vision. The meeting lasted every bit of 17 minutes. After that phone call, I sat in my office chair in disbelief. *Did I just get commissioned to do a book cover for Laura Di Franco? Did we just have a meeting about her upcoming book, which was coming out in a few months?*

This meant I didn't have time to play around with procrastination, which loves to be in my business!

Fast forward a couple of months.

Hey Laura, here is a mock-up of the book cover. Let me know your thoughts," I said.

It didn't take her long to reply.

"I love it! Can you make these small changes so I can put it up on Facebook for the other authors to see it?"

I was so excited she loved the design! I did a happy dance and everything! The book title is *100 Poems & Possibilities for Healing;* look it up and check out my design. By the way, it also achieved a number-one bestseller on Amazon in multiple categories!

I create designs that aren't only visually stunning but also meaningful and impactful. The journey from concept to completion is a blend of creativity, strategy, and collaboration, resulting in artwork that stands out and resonates deeply with its audience.

The journey to this point has been anything but linear. Each step, struggle, and victory shaped my approach to design and to life. Looking back, I realize my years of frustration and side hustles weren't wasted. They were integral to my growth and to finding my true calling.

Becoming a single mom of three children while holding a stable government job offered a sense of security, but my heart was always elsewhere. The turning point with Laura wasn't just a professional milestone but a personal awakening. It was a testament to perseverance and to the importance of seizing opportunities when they finally arise.

My role as a Creative Specialist evolved. I'm no longer just a designer; I'm a storyteller. Each project I undertake is a new story waiting to be told, a new emotion waiting to be captured. And with each story, I learn something new about myself and the world around me.

I still have moments of self-doubt. I still face challenges that test my resolve. But now, I embrace them with a new perspective. I know that every closed door is not the end but a redirection to something greater. Every setback is a setup for a comeback.

To anyone reading this who's struggling with their own journey, remember that your story is still being written. Embrace every chapter, even the difficult ones. They're all part of the masterpiece that is your life.

Let me take you on a journey into my mind when it comes to creating beautiful works of art that aren't only worthy of the world to see but also explain the important things you should look out for when creating eye-catching designs. Below are some strategies you can follow to make eye-catching designs for your next project.

The Strategy

Creating a masterpiece involves more than talent; it requires vision, passion, and attention to detail. Here are the key elements I focus on when crafting a design that stands out:

1. Understanding the Vision

The first step is to fully grasp the client's vision. What message do they want to convey? What emotions should the design evoke? This involves asking the right questions and actively listening. I will start by discussing the project's goals and the client's preferences. This could mean understanding the tone of a book, the brand's personality, or the intended impact of a mural. It's essential to capture the essence of what the client envisions and translate that into a visual representation.

2. Research and Inspiration

Once I understand the vision, I dive into research. I look at current design trends, study the target audience, and gather inspiration from various sources. This helps me create a design that's both relevant and unique. Research might involve looking at competitors, exploring different artistic styles, and understanding the cultural context. Inspiration can come from nature, art galleries, everyday life, or even a conversation with a friend. The goal is to fill my creative well with diverse and rich ideas.

3. Concept Development

I start with rough sketches and brainstorm different concepts. This is where creativity flows freely, and I explore various ideas without constraints. The goal is to generate multiple options to find the best fit. This stage is experimental and playful. I might create several versions of a design, each with a different approach. It's about pushing boundaries and thinking outside the box to find the most compelling visual solution.

4. Attention to Detail

Details make the design. From the choice of colors to typography and layout, every element must harmonize to create a cohesive and appealing design. Consistency and precision are crucial. This means paying close attention to spacing, alignment, and balance. Each detail, no matter how small, contributes to the overall effectiveness and beauty of the design. It's about crafting something that feels polished and well-considered.

5. Feedback and Revisions

Collaboration with the client is key. I present my concepts and welcome feedback. This iterative process ensures the final design aligns perfectly with the client's vision. I see feedback as a valuable part of the creative process. It helps refine and improve the design, making sure it meets the client's expectations and objectives. This stage may involve multiple rounds of revisions, but each one brings the design closer to perfection.

6. Emotional Connection

The best designs resonate emotionally with the audience. Whether it's a sense of nostalgia, excitement, or tranquility, the design should evoke the desired emotional response. I aim to create visuals that connect with people on a deeper level. This involves understanding the psychology of colors, the power of imagery, and the impact of composition. A successful design isn't just seen; it's felt.

7. Practicality and Usability

A design must be not only beautiful but also practical. It should serve its purpose effectively, whether it's a book cover, a mural, or a website. Usability and functionality are just as important as aesthetics. This means considering how the design will be used and ensuring it's accessible and user-friendly. For example, a book cover needs to be readable at various sizes, while a website should be easy to navigate.

8. Using High-Quality Images

High-quality images are essential for creating a professional look. Invest in good photography or work with skilled designers to ensure your visuals are top-notch. Poor-quality images can harm your brand's reputation and turn potential customers away.

9. Storytelling

Every design tells a story. It should capture and convey the essence of the subject, drawing the viewer into a visual narrative that leaves a lasting impression. Storytelling in design involves creating a journey for the viewer. It might be a sequence of images, a compelling focal point, or a clever use of metaphors. The aim is to engage the audience and make the design memorable.

Thank you for joining me on this journey. Remember, every design tells a story, and every artist has a unique way of telling it. What's your story? Embrace your path, overcome your doubts, and create your visual business masterpiece that not only establishes your identity but also sells. Your journey, with all its twists and turns, is leading you to where you need to be. Trust the process and keep creating.

Tanya Stokes, a vibrant spirit originally from Washington, D.C., but molded by the serene life of Lanham, Maryland, proudly holds membership in the esteemed and altruistic sorority Sigma Gamma Rho, showcasing her dedication to community and excellence.

Her academic journey reached impressive heights with an MBA in Computer Networking in 2007 and an MPA in Public Administration in 2014, both from Strayer University. Yet, despite her mastery in these fields, her heart resonated elsewhere.

In the enthralling world of graphic design, Tanya unearthed her true calling. She discovered profound joy in bringing customers' aspirations to life through the art of crafting mesmerizing business logos, dynamic business cards, captivating book covers, and innovative websites catered to small businesses.

In a bold move in 2018, she founded her brainchild, Compassionate Design LLC. The name, adorned with "Compassionate," reflects her philosophy—a philosophy that echoes deeply in her design concepts. Rather than conjuring ideas from thin air, she delves into the core of her clients' visions, nurturing a profound understanding of their desires. Her commitment lies not just in creating products but in making her clients' imaginations into tangible designs.

Fueled by her indomitable spirit, she embarked on yet another audacious journey, founding Compassionate Designs Publishing. It all began with an author seeking publication avenues at a fraction of the industry's cost. Driven by this encounter, Tanya vowed to provide publishing services to aspiring authors, championing their stories with affordability and passion. Her motto resounds with inspiration: "There is a book in everyone—make time to write it out and publish it."

Tanya's artistic endeavors extend beyond design; she is the author of two poetry books, *The Truth* and *My Muse*. Additionally, she co-authored three books: *100 Poems and Possibilities of Healing*, *Occupy*, and *The Miss Adventures Guide to Ultimate Empowerment for Women*. These literary works are a testament to her multifaceted creativity and dedication to artistic expression.

Connect with Tanya:

Website: https://compassionate-designs.com/

Website: https://www.amazon.com/author/tanya.stokes

Email: tanya.stokes@compassionate-designs.com

Chapter 16

Mastering Instagram

Engagement Strategies that Attract Perfect Clients

María del Mar Oliva

> It's not the algorithm; it's you!

My Story

Listen closely: *98% of my business comes from Instagram, and I've met 98% of my friends on Instagram.*

Read that again.

I repeat that line weekly during speaking engagements, networking meetings, and conversations with my colleagues. Sometimes, I want to scream it from the rooftops.

I learned the power of community back in Puerto Rico, as being born and raised in a small town in the Southeastern portion of the island wasn't easy. Everyone knows each other, and the town gossip travels faster than Amazon Prime deliveries.

It was hard to grow up in a town where everyone knew who I was — I felt like I had a scarlet letter permanently sewn to my chest.

However, as I grew older, I realized that attention came from a place of care and how beautiful it was that a town full of bodyguards cared enough to watch me grow up and have my back through it all.

I was looking for this sense of community in 2017 after leaving a post-Hurricane Maria-ridden Puerto Rico and landing in the D.C. Metro area, but I had no luck.

I remember walking down the airplane aisle and thinking: *I'm outgoing and friendly. I'm sure I won't have any trouble finding new friends in the States. It'll all work itself out.*

Tick tock. Tick tock. It's been five years, and I still haven't found any friends.

What the Hell is going on?

Am I boring?

Am I not good enough?

Will I be lonely forever?

I miss Puerto Rico.

During the first 1,825 lonesome days I lived in the United States, my family reassured me, "Marí, you'll be fine. You'll find friends in no time! You just have to be patient."

Looking back, I believe there were multiple reasons why I didn't make any meaningful connections during that time.

Reason #1: I just didn't fit in—and it sucked.

I didn't eat the same food or listen to the same music, and English was not my first language. When I tried to make meaningful connections with others, it was obvious we didn't have much in common. Their jokes didn't make sense to me, and my jokes didn't make sense to them. Hell, we didn't even watch many of the same TV shows growing up—I watched *Friends* for the first time in 2023—yeah, I said it.

Reason #2: I was late to the party—and it showed.

Moving at 21 was challenging. Everyone I met seemed to have a solid group of friends, and they weren't accepting new members.

Why don't they invite me out with their other friends?

I guess we're just work friends?

Why don't they want me to be part of their group?

Ugh, I miss my friends back home.

I spiraled through these thoughts at least once a week for five years.

Reason #3: I chose to live in D.C., of all places.

Living in the D.C. area has its disadvantages. Everyone's busy all the time, and social calendars are booked weeks, months, or seasons in advance. It was a complete 180-degree change from the spontaneity I was used to. I ran into the same scenarios over and over again.

Me: "Hey, I loved meeting you on Tuesday. Would you be willing to meet again soon to grab some coffee or drinks?"

Them: "Hey María! Yes, I'd love to meet for coffee soon. Maybe in January?"

But it's September! I have no idea what I will be doing next week, let alone January.

"Sure, that'd be great," I said anyway.

Spoiler alert: The coffee meetup never happened!

Me: "Hi, friend. I'd love to see you again soon. Let me know when you're available!"

Them: "Hey, girl! I'd love to meet up soon, too. I have so much going on, but I can do something in three weeks. How does that sound?"

Wait what? There's no way she's not available until then. This doesn't happen in Puerto Rico. We make same-day plans an hour in advance. We make time for each other. This is so weird!

"Sounds good, let's meet then!" I sighed as I clicked send.

Spoiler alert: We indeed did not meet!

I accommodated and adjusted to the social environment that consistently pushed me aside.

Reason #4: And then, COVID hit.

As a very extroverted human, it drove me crazy sitting at home on my computer for days with minimal social interaction.

How long has it been? Two minutes? It feels like hours.

I can't wait for this craziness to be over.

How am I going to make friends now?

I need to talk to someone before I start crawling up the walls!

These feelings and a lot of soul-searching made me realize I needed an escape. Whether it was a part-time job, a side hustle, or joining a gym—I needed to be social ASAP.

Then, six months after the first lockdown, I pursued social media management on my own and launched SMS Media.

I also enrolled in a social media management course that changed my life forever. It taught me the power of community engagement and how much it can make or break a small business's social media efforts.

During my studies as an undergrad, I learned many marketing concepts. I thought I had read, heard, and seen everything from buyer psychology, paid ads, sales funnels, email marketing, automation, and content writing.

But then, one afternoon, I heard my coach say, "Your ideal client wants to feel seen, heard, understood, and validated. They want to interact with the person behind the logo, they want to see who you are unfiltered, and when they feel like they know you on a more personal level, it'll be a no-brainer for them to want to work with you, too."

It made sense because this happened to me with my favorite restaurants in town. The ones that respond to my comments or stories make me feel special. The ones that don't make me not want to visit them again.

It all started to make sense. Instagram marketing is much more than choosing a pretty picture and adding a quote as a caption. It's all about building genuine connections.

I started leaning into these principles, and the direct messages started flowing, my posts got many more comments, and I landed my first social media management client before I reached 100 followers.

Mind-blowing, I know—it's funny how something so simple worked so perfectly.

I feel seen.

I feel accepted.

I feel like myself again.

They like me.

They accept me.

They're laughing with me and not at me.

I can't believe it. It's finally happening. I've found my Puerto Rico in the US.

I'm so grateful.

I sat down in my bed one night, and tears rolled down my cheeks. My heart beat fast, and my eyes stared at the bright light of my phone screen as the direct message notifications flooded in.

Replies to my Instagram stories turned into deep conversations in the DMs about life, business, partners, and our hate for coffee.

These conversations turned into in-person meetings, lunches, and invites to networking events.

I left each event with a new friend!

These friends began to refer me to others, collaboration opportunities, introductions, and the golden ticket—more paying clients.

The only feeling that beats this one is waking up thinking, *OMG, I didn't hear my alarm!* to realize it's Saturday, and you have nowhere to go.

We all know being an entrepreneur can be a lonely journey, but it doesn't have to be. This is your sign to lean into your online community and stop blaming the algorithm because it's not the algorithm; it's you!

Like Donnie Boivin once said, "Do not put yourself on an island."

There are people out there who need and want you and are searching for someone exactly like you.

And yes, it will be uncomfortable at first, but that's what being an entrepreneur is all about. So, buckle up and enjoy the ride!

The Strategy

Engage Like a Pro in 30 Minutes

Contrary to popular belief, Instagram marketing can indeed be simple, easy, and fun.

No matter what new features, algorithm updates, or trends pop up, one thing will always be true: We have to be social on social media to see results.

Treat your Instagram as a virtual networking event where you can show up any time or day you like, and you'll quickly attract perfect clients.

Imagine you walk into a networking event. You skim the room in hopes of finding something in common with someone—their drink of choice or outfit style.

You see someone that's wearing a jersey from your alma mater. You take a big sip of your drink, unclench your jaw, and make very heavy steps to make your way to them.

They look at you, and you smile: "Hi, so nice to meet you; I'm [your name]. I noticed you're wearing a [your alma mater] jersey. Did you go there too? I graduated in 2014!"

And—no response. They just roll their eyes, take a sip of their drink, and move away. How would you feel?

Ignored?

Unheard?

Embarrassed?

Angry?

Unwanted?

That's exactly how your Instagram followers feel when you ignore their comments and direct messages (DMs). You don't want them to feel this way.

You want them to feel like you're accessible, helpful, a friend, nice, respectful, and kind.

You want them to want to continue commenting on your content and start building a genuine relationship with them.

Here's how to achieve this:

Step 1: Find a quiet and comfortable space free from distractions. Set your phone to silent, close your computer, and tell your friends and family you're unavailable for 30 minutes.

Now, set a ten-minute timer on your phone or watch. Open the Instagram app and begin interacting with posts that appear on your feed.

DO:

- Look at the image(s) and read the caption carefully.
- Ask yourself, "Do I like this content? If yes, like and comment on it. If not, skip it!
- Ask yourself, "Does it inspire me to comment or ask a question?" If yes, like and comment on it. If not, skip it!
- Make meaningful comments that reiterate what the author is talking about or in which you act with follow-up questions to start a conversation with them.

DON'T:

- Make general comments such as "Awesome," "Looks great," or even "Great tips."
- Cold pitch or self-promote your product or service to anyone who hasn't shown interest.
- Make every interaction about you. Instead, make it about them.

Bonus tip: It can take a small business owner up to four hours to create one piece of content. Therefore, general comments without value or acknowledgment of their message will be considered disrespectful and inconsiderate.

Here's a client example: Steve is a CPA who works mainly with small business owners nationwide. On Tuesday, he posted a professional headshot of himself with the following caption:

"REMINDER FOR SMALL BUSINESS OWNERS

Quarterly taxes are due next Thursday at 11:59 p.m. EST. Remember to make your payments to avoid penalties and fines.

Have any questions? Drop them below!"

His post got three comments. Let's analyze them together.

- @susant: "Looking good, Steve"
- @claudiaponz: "Thank you for the reminder, Steve. I always forget to pay my quarterly taxes. Do you have any recommendations on how to calculate what my quarterly tax payments should be?"
- @juancarlos: "My man, thank you for the tip."

Which comment do you think was the best? If you said Claudia Ponz's comment was the best, you're correct.

Why? Claudia acknowledged Steve's tip, got vulnerable about her struggles, and made a follow-up question for Steve to answer.

This interaction could become an opportunity for Steve to build Claudia's trust by giving her the recommendation she asked for.

He can also respond to her privately and start a conversation there to provide her with free tips and tricks. If he offers a quarterly tax calculation service, he could potentially turn Claudia into a paying client for his business.

Don't be Susan or Juan on Instagram; be a Claudia!

Step 2: Once the first timer goes off, set it up for another ten minutes. This time, you'll interact with your audience's stories.

You'll find your audience's stories in a horizontal line of circles at the top of your Instagram feed. Each circle represents a Story posted by someone you follow.

Tap on the first circle you see from left to right and:

- Observe the image or video.
- Listen to what they're saying.
- Ask yourself: What topic are they talking about?
- Make a meaningful comment related to the image, video, or topic they're discussing. You'll also get brownie points if you ask a question.

When in doubt, follow the do's and don'ts mentioned above, and remember to skip any post that doesn't inspire you.

Step 3: Now, set your timer to five minutes. This time focus on a fun outbound marketing tactic. Outbound marketing is when a business reaches out to potential ideal clients to get them interested in their product or service.

You'll find a hashtag your ideal clients use to find the product or service you're looking for.

Then, you'll search for that hashtag and click on it. Once you see a grid view on your screen, find a post that stands out.

Read the caption, look at the image or Reel, and make a genuine comment referring to the caption and image.

I'll give you an example.

Mark is a real estate photographer in the Washington, D.C. area. His ideal clients are luxury real estate professionals who need professional pictures of their listings to attract ideal buyers in 60 days or less.

His ideal clients spend their free time at networking events, fine dining, wineries, breweries, luxury shopping, or traveling. Here's a list of hashtags Mark interacts with every week:

- #dcrealestate
- #dmvrealestate
- #dcrealtor
- #dcrealestateagents
- #dcluxuryrealestate
- #dcrealtor
- #dcluxuryhomes
- #dcrestaurants
- #dcfinedining
- #dcluxury

Make a list of ten hashtags that describe your ideal clients and where they're spending their free time, just like Mark did.

This tactic is extremely successful because it teaches the algorithm exactly who you want to interact with, meaning that it will show you more of the same accounts.

Secondly, it will increase your account engagement. Don't forget that we have to be social to see results on social media.

When you interact with others, they naturally want to interact with you. It's a win-win situation. This is how you build genuine connections and attract ideal clients.

Q: "Do I need to follow them?"
A: Not unless you genuinely want to.

Q: "Won't it be weird if I comment on their content but don't follow them?"
A: If they already have their profile public, it won't be weird. I promise.

Step 4: Lastly, set your timer to five minutes and focus on answering comments made on your posts and direct messages you have received.

This is the most important step of the community engagement process. Why? To build a community that knows, likes, and trusts you, it's important that they feel reciprocated, seen, heard, and understood by you.

They also want to see your personality. Who are you outside of your business? Do you drink coffee or tea every morning? Are you a bookworm or a movie watcher?

Before you start getting nervous, you don't have to make your Instagram your reality TV show. However, you do need to share glimpses of the person behind the pretty logo, font, and colors.

It's up to you how much you share. You can pick 1 to 3 of the items below and start sharing more of them every week.

- Your morning routine
- Daily work-to-do list
- Favorite TV show
- Preferred cocktail or a bit of your story if you don't drink
- Your hobbies
- Local restaurant recommendations
- Behind the scenes of a business process
- Go to local businesses to support
- Staff introductions or highlights
- A day in the life at your business
- Unboxing new supplies or products (non-branded)
- Favorite books or podcasts

- Celebrating business milestones or anniversaries
- Polls or questions to engage followers
- Inspirational quotes or motivational messages
- Fun facts about your industry
- Your workspace or office setup
- Sharing your pet or plants
- Industry tips, tricks, or misconceptions
- When you prioritize building connections, pouring into others, and being authentic on Instagram, you'll understand the power you have and how what goes around comes around. And what's in store for you is an abundance of perfectly aligned paying clients.

Don't say I didn't warn you! It was not the algorithm; it was you!

María del Mar Oliva is the CEO of SMS Media, a social media agency that helps service providers get discovered, build strong communities, and attract leads via sustainable Instagram strategies. She has over nine years of experience in digital marketing.

She has helped hundreds of businesses worldwide find ways to make social media work around their lifestyles, have fun when creating content, feel excited to show up online, and implement fun, sustainable, and simple strategies.

Her mission? To make social media less scary and more fun for everyone. María's all about keeping it real and keeping it light. She's your go-to gal for practical tips and tricks that work, delivered with a side of humor and a lot of heart.

When María is not working, you can find her binge-watching a Bravo reality TV show, having some lechón in her hometown in Puerto Rico, baking some chocolate chip cookies, or (this one is the most likely, honestly) at a nearby happy hour sipping some Pinot Grigio, white sangria, or a very gingery Moscow Mule.

Connect with María:

Instagram: https://www.instagram.com/mariaolivasocial/
Pick Her Brain: https://calendly.com/maria_oliva/pick-my-brain
Website: https://smsmediapr.lpages.co/services/
LinkedIn: https://www.linkedin.com/in/mariaoliva13/
Glossary
*Interacting = liking, commenting, saving, or sharing someone's content

Chapter 17

Leverage Up on LinkedIn
Magnify Visibility and Attract the Right Clients
Deanna Russo

> *It doesn't have to be overwhelming.*
> *It doesn't have to be a place*
> *where only certain people hang out.*
> *It doesn't have to be just for job seekers.*
> *You can make LinkedIn work for you and your goals.*
> *You can use LinkedIn to bring in business!*

I did it. I "cold call" pitched strangers on LinkedIn. I did it for a couple of months,

until...

...There has got to be a better way. How would these people work with a stranger who pitched them?

You don't have to pitch. You can create the know, like, and trust factor on LinkedIn, and you will see your business magnify the way you want it to and attract the people who need you and your products and services.

My Story

My boss: "Congratulations, welcome to the team!"

Me: "Thank you. I'm very excited about this opportunity."

My boss: "We want you to use LinkedIn to bring in new clients."

Me: "Okay, I already have a LinkedIn account, but I haven't been super active on it. I will figure it out."

My boss: "Good. We want you to write a script and send that same script to companies in direct messages and emails."

I did what I was told. I wrote up a script. I sent it to people at companies. I did it over and over again. I got little to no response.

Then my lightbulb moment hit: *They don't know me, they don't like me, and they really don't trust me. I need to change how I approach LinkedIn.*

Back then, I was a married mom of three kids eight years old and under, working in my second sales job ever, at a small IT start-up, in a city I had just moved to a year before. My boss wanted me to use LinkedIn as the primary way to bring in business. I could do this. I brought ten years of social media and content marketing experience to that sales role.

I'm determined to make this work.

I needed clients. If I changed my strategy, what was the guarantee that it would work? There is no guarantee. Few things in life have a guarantee.

I was willing to take the risk, pitching wasn't working, and I needed a better way to get this done. My job was to make money for the company.

My triangle strategy began when I considered my ultimate goal and what I was doing to achieve that goal up until that point. Then I thought about what I could do differently that worked for me and worked for the end goal - getting clients.

I committed myself to the triangle strategy I created. I based it on profile, engagement, and content, and it changed the way I approached LinkedIn.

Before that sales job, I had a LinkedIn account for ten years, but I treated it like an online resume. I never did anything with it. If I changed jobs, I'd update my work experience, but that was it. My profile was a shell of who I was.

Instead of pitching or an online resume, I changed how I thought about the platform—I started to think about and treat LinkedIn like a big networking event.

All these strangers on LinkedIn need to know me. All these strangers on LinkedIn need to like me. All these strangers on LinkedIn need to trust me. Then the strangers won't be strangers anymore, they'll be prospects, referral partners, and clients.

The triangle strategy converted the know, like, and trust to tangible things I could do on LinkedIn, which helped me grow from 400-11,000 followers in 18 months.

As I'm writing this chapter, I now have close to 30,000+ followers on LinkedIn.

That includes clients, referral partners, collaborators, the list goes on and on. Half of the clients I've worked with since I started my company have come directly from LinkedIn.

A year and a half after I taught myself the triangle strategy, I started teaching it to other people.

The strategy I created that takes the pitch out of the equation and transforms how you treat the LinkedIn platform, is made up of profile, engagement, and content. Let's break it all down and I'll show you how it works!

The Strategy

Instead of cold-call pitching to attract new clients and customers, picture this: LinkedIn is a big networking event, except it's a networking event with one billion people in attendance. Like a face-to-face networking event, we're there to get to know each other, like each other, and trust each other.

It boils down to getting to know people through your LinkedIn profile, getting to like people through your LinkedIn engagement (comments lead to conversations), and building trust through your LinkedIn content.

Before you get ready to get to work on all of the above, you need to answer some questions:

Why am I on LinkedIn?

You may be a business owner, or you work for a small business where LinkedIn is a key part of your marketing and sales strategy.

It's important to make it clear to people in your profile, comments, and content why you're on the platform.

Sure, it's social media, but why are you really on LinkedIn? Are you on the platform to build relationships? Are you on LinkedIn to learn?

What is your ultimate goal?

Who is my target audience?

Who are you trying to reach? Who is your ideal client? What are the demographics that make up that ideal client?

Knowing who the person is that you're trying to reach makes a **huge** difference because you know who you want to talk to.

Who am I?

What brought you to where you are now? What's your story? What's your differentiator? What sets you apart from everyone else who does what you do?

If you can answer these questions, awesome!

Sell yourself to us by relating to us; it's not about you; it's about the people you help!

Having the answers to those questions before you start all the work will help you sell yourself on LinkedIn without pitching. Yes, it can be done!

Those answers will also help you attract the right clients, the people you want to work with, and those who have the money to work with you.

Dig deep and get the questions answered before preparing to do the work and converting that work to my triangle strategy.

Okay, got those answers? Ready, set, let's go!

Leverage Up Your LinkedIn Profile

Before you walk into a networking event, do you check the mirror to see how you look, what you're wearing, and how you present yourself? Probably. LinkedIn is a big networking event—huge.

Your LinkedIn profile is the foundation of everything you do. It's the first part of my triangle strategy and the concrete the house is built on. You can't install doors and windows on that house if the foundation hasn't been completed yet. The doors and windows on LinkedIn are all the extras like LinkedIn Premium or LinkedIn Sales Navigator. You don't need to pay for LinkedIn to get all the benefits that come with it.

Everything you do on LinkedIn comes back to your profile. When you comment, people go to your profile to look at you. When you post content, people go to your profile to look at you. Without a strong profile that answers, "Who are you?" "What do you do?" and "Who do you serve?" you're leaving more questions than answers. Do you want people to guess what you do? Do you want people to guess how you help people? They won't guess. They'll scroll by without thinking twice.

You should be very proud of each part of your LinkedIn profile, from your profile picture to your banner image, to your About section, and even your Experience section. As you complete each section, you should feel excited about what you're putting out there for the masses to see.

As you work on each section, remove the "LinkedIn is an online resume" phrase from your vocabulary. Yes, many people treated the platform that way when it launched in 2003 and for years afterward, but that's no longer the case.

LinkedIn is a big networking event. If you aren't smiling in your profile picture, or we can't see your face, how can we get to know you? Do you go into a networking event with an angry face? Probably not. You go into that room and smile. That's the person we want to meet!

The circle LinkedIn gives you for your profile picture is not a big one. It's even smaller when you're using the LinkedIn mobile app. Don't use a full body picture as your LinkedIn profile picture. We want to see your face and your smile, so a head and shoulders shot works better.

Your headline isn't your job title. There are millions of account executives on LinkedIn. There are millions of project managers on LinkedIn. What sets one project manager apart from another? Your LinkedIn headline will blend in with everyone else who's on LinkedIn IF you continue to use a job title. That goes for business owners, too. Instead, make your headline a phrase or series of phrases that tell people what you do and who you serve, what makes you unique.

Use a clear and concise banner image with text that answers: "Who am I and what do I do?" and an About section that people can relate to and that tells a story about you and that shares your why.

There should be no doubt in the reader's mind about who you are, who you serve, and what you do after visiting your LinkedIn profile. Each section, from your banner to your recommendations, should answer all the questions.

Write it in the first person not the third. It's you talking about yourself. My profile isn't Deanna Russo talking about Deanna Russo; it's me talking about who I am, what I do, and who I serve.

Leverage Up Your LinkedIn Engagement

Have you ever walked into a networking event and noticed that everyone was giving each other a thumbs-up? Yeah, me neither. If I witnessed that, I'd probably turn around and walk out of the event. That would be strange and awkward.

Have you ever walked into a face-to-face networking event and observed signs hanging from the rafters telling you what the topics of those conversations were?

Me neither. I'd *love* to see that, though.

That's the metaphor I use when I teach strategic engagement on LinkedIn. It's the second part of my triangle strategy. It's about going to the conversations where you know you want to be visible.

Going to those conversations on LinkedIn means it's not just you scrolling through your home feed, finding things to comment on, and hoping and praying someone sees it. Instead, you're strategically going to other conversations because you know, "Those are my people; I can jump in and share my knowledge."

You know those are the people who'll buy from you - your ideal clients. You know those are the people who you want to be more visible to.

When you're having conversations with people, you're using words to communicate. The same thing goes for LinkedIn. When you react to content using the thumbs up, heart, support, or clapping emojis, we can't get to like you if we can't have conversations with you. We can't get to like you if all you're doing is reacting.

Have conversations in the comments and talk to people the way you would face to face because those people will like and relate to you when you interact and respond. It's just like having a conversation in person; there should be a back and forth.

Commenting is also important because LinkedIn is a massively large spider web that connects you to other people who may be able to relate and what you're saying. If I comment on John's post, he's not the only one who sees my comments. He sees them, *and* so do his followers and connections (your second-degree connections), and never underestimate those third-degree connections. Multiple degrees of people see your interactions and comments.

Here's another way to look at it: your LinkedIn profile is a billboard. Would you rather have that billboard standing along a desolate road that no cars travel on, or would you rather have that billboard erected along a bustling highway that lots of cars see? When you comment, you take that billboard to the busy highway and make your profile more visible to the masses.

You attract people and allow them to like you and relate to you, and you become much more visible in the process.

Have conversations because the more you do it, the more you'll realize that commenting is fun.

Leverage Up Your LinkedIn Content

When you talk to people at a networking event and explain what you do, why you do it, or a client's success story, do people pay more attention to you? Does your energy shine through that story? Do people see your enthusiasm?

If you answered yes to any or all of the above, you should share what you do with the masses, not just people you come into contact with face to face.

Why aren't you sharing what you do, taking people behind the scenes, or sharing the client success stories with people on LinkedIn? Is it because you're worried about what other people think? Is it because you don't think people care?

Let me be the first to tell you people do care. People care because they want to get to know you better. They want to trust you. Content is the third part of my triangle strategy.

It's time to share the stories and behind-the-scenes tales that only you know.

It's time to earn the trust of people who may and will become clients. You can't earn that trust if you use lingo or algorithms that go over our heads. When you post on LinkedIn, use words everyone will understand.

Do you know what the best part of sharing content on LinkedIn is? If you post content, you'll stand out because even though there are one billion people on the platform, only a very small percentage share content. That means you have plenty of room to get your message out.

Content on LinkedIn should not be salesy or spammy. That doesn't mean you shouldn't talk about what you want people to know regarding your business. That being said, there's a good balance between sharing the important stuff (your event that's coming up or the book you're ready to publish that you want everyone to know about) and stories that take us behind the scenes of what you're doing and your business.

To trust you with our business, we need to get to know you, the business owner.

If all you're doing is selling us with your content, we can't get to know the person who is sweating it out and working extra hours to make sure the lights stay on. If all you're doing is selling us with your content, we can't get to know the person who runs his or her business because they love what they do.

When it comes to content, consistency needs to be underlined and bolded. When I started creating content on LinkedIn, I only posted twice a week—that's it. The thing is, I kept that up for over a year. You don't have to post every single day of the week. You don't have to post five days a week.

Content on LinkedIn is like fine wine. It needs time to marinate, to breathe. I often see posts in my feed that are a day, two, or three old. That's okay; I still comment on them.

Even though I don't recommend posting content seven days a week, I do recommend consistently showing up on LinkedIn. Comment on the days you aren't posting. That commenting window doesn't have to be a large one; 15 to 30 minutes usually does the trick.

The triangle strategy I created for clients includes profile, engagement, and content. If I were to transform that triangle into a square or a rectangle, the fourth piece would be consistency. Showing up consistently is just as important as what you say in your profile, what you say in your comments, and what you say in your content.

By ensuring you have a strong LinkedIn profile that answers all the questions, we can get to know you. By having conversations in the comments, we can get to like you. By posting content that showcases your value, we build trust with you.

By consistently doing all of the above, we can do business with you—that's what it's all about.

Deanna Russo grew her LinkedIn network independently from 400 to 30,000+ followers.

She started Leverage Up to pass on her knowledge of LinkedIn and help others achieve all the benefits she learned.

She has a distinct LinkedIn strategy made up of three parts called her LinkedIn triangle. It's made up of profile, engagement, and content. There is a link between each part of that triangle and once you're successful in one part, you need the other two parts for a good balance. You can't have one piece without the other two.

Deanna works with her one-on-one clients and corporate clients to maximize the benefits of LinkedIn in the fastest way possible getting the fundamentals down before wasting time and money on all the extras LinkedIn offers. She helps her clients brand themselves, boost visibility, and have conversations that directly lead to business.

Outside of her business, Deanna is a married mom of three and a huge Buffalo Bills fan.

Connect with Deanna:

Website and Email Blast Sign-Up: https://leverageupllc.com/
LinkedIn Profile: https://www.linkedin.com/in/deannarusso1/
Facebook: https://www.facebook.com/deanna.russo.leverage.up

Chapter 18

Demystifying Video for Business Development
Consciously Creating Reality with Your Thoughts
Kyle Steinle

> *I would find myself curled up in the fetal position on the basement floor, attempting to escape from the world, at times wishing for death. Wouldn't that be easier?*

My Story

Do you ever scare people into working with you?

Or do they come to you out of love?

Your own thoughts make all the difference!

Depending on whether those thoughts are based in fear or in love directly correlates to the feeling you create for yourself and for your audience.

Realizing the power of my thoughts started at 3 a.m. on November 15, 2017, when I awoke to loud banging on the front door. I pulled back the blackout curtain covering the bedroom window to see red and blue lights; two police cars sat in front of our home.

What the hell is this about? Am I in trouble?

The walls seemed to shake as I nervously turned on the hallway light—*BANG BANG BANG*—again on the front door. I made my way downstairs to find two police officers.

"Are you Kyle Steinle?"

"Yes."

"Are you the son of Steve Steinle?"

"Yes."

"Can we come in?"

Oh no, this can't be good. Is my dad okay?

"Kyle, we're sorry to tell you, but your father was found dead this evening at his home."

WHAT?

"I...I don't know what to say."

Overcome by shock and surprise, I remember feeling frozen, the police officers staring at me, waiting for an emotional reaction. When it didn't come, I felt scared, like they suspected me of something.

"The detective will call soon to speak with you."

Why is there a detective?

"Okay."

The officers left. I turned to Jen, my girlfriend, now wife, as the realization that my father died hit me like a ton of bricks. I completely broke down, hugging Jen as I began to sob uncontrollably on her shoulder.

Eventually, the detective called around 4 a.m., explaining that my father had died of a cocaine overdose, and they suspected fentanyl would show up in the toxicology report as well, which it did.

"There were two individuals with him at home; they attempted to administer NARCAN, and they have both been arrested on outstanding warrants."

I told him to kick those assholes out! I knew they were no good!

The next day, I went to my dad's house, scared and anxious about what I might find. It was a mess, like a bomb had gone off. The entire place was turned inside out.

Did the police do this? What happened here?

It looked like a frat house that had been raided. Clearly, a lot of partying had gone on—empty liquor and beer bottles, ashtrays full of cigarette butts. There were clear signs of searching, most likely by the police.

As I nervously made my way through my father's home, surveying the atrocity, two things struck me. The first was an 8x10 picture of me, from the day of my high school graduation, shaking the principal's hand on stage. He had clearly been doing lines of cocaine on it.

What a fucking scene. Am I dreaming? Is this even real?

Making my way downstairs, past the bar toward the sunroom outback, was the board game "Sorry." It jumped out at me in such a way that I felt it was him telling me just that, "Sorry, Kyle."

The rest of my survey included discovering blood splatter on walls and ceilings and items too disturbing to include here.

How did I not know all this was going on in my dad's life?

This was the beginning of my entrepreneurial journey, less than two months after I took the leap of faith and resigned from my nine-to-five at the University.

Here I was, trying to figure out the direction of my business while feeling emotionally devastated. Not to mention confused, as I was hurled into administering an estate going through probate for the first time. On top of that, I was now my grandmother's caregiver, a role my father played as her only child.

Fuck me.

This was the general theme of the thoughts I had.

I am never going to figure all this out. I can't do this. This is too much. I hate my life. Why me?

So much negativity, fear, doubt, worry—all the horrible, scary thoughts ran through my head daily. I literally created a personal Hell for myself with so much inner torment and terror. Many times, I broke down and fell to my knees crying or curled up in a fetal position on the basement floor, attempting to escape from the world and, at times, wishing for death. *Wouldn't that be easier?*

This must be what Hell feels like. And there's no escape.

As I muddled through, I eventually established my business and remembered the reason I decided to embark on this entrepreneurial journey. It was several years earlier when I made a conscious decision to "do good."

Flashback to 2014—life was easy and fun at the University, yet for some reason, unfulfilling.

I realized I accomplished everything I was told I was "supposed to do" growing up. I had a good job, a house, a car, and health insurance—I was secure! So why did I feel something was missing?

I dug into self-reflection and realized I wanted something more, and something more was waiting for me. The only conclusion I had then was that I wanted to "do good" with my life. After making that choice, in the years leading up to my father's death, I began to find out what that meant. I uncovered a deeper spiritual side of life through meditation practice, sound healing, and a variety of other healing modalities.

"Doing good" became more than just something to do; it became a state of being, a way to live life. Such that anything done from this state would be done with love and, thus, done "good."

When my dad died, it was like the biggest test to start applying what I learned in my spiritual practices.

When I found myself wishing for death and an ending to my inner personal Hell, I reached into my spiritual tool bag. I asked, "What am I afraid of?"

Through unpacking my negative thoughts, I discovered the source was always fear. I learned that any negative thought, whether it be anger or depression, always had a source of fear. Once I became aware of this, I re-wrote the internal script and began to craft new thoughts from a more positive place.

This didn't happen overnight. It took years of practice and continues to. However, I find that if I'm honest with myself, and choose to think positively, I can change the negative thoughts into positive ones. This, most importantly, changes my negative *feelings* into positive ones.

So, when it comes to my video business, I decided to create videos that share messages based on love and positivity. Inevitably, this created a positive response from my clients.

Now, it's time for you to take control of your own thoughts to create a positive reality for yourself and *your* audience.

The Strategy

Part 1 – The Special Powers

Have you ever been so completely absorbed by a movie or TV show that you completely forgot about your own life?

Has your body ever tensed up during the fight scene of an action movie? Have you ever cried during a particularly emotionally painful scene of a drama?

This is the special power of video!

It's the power to literally transport you to a new reality. For just a moment, you're feeling the feelings of the reality on screen. It feels like you're there! How does this happen?

As you may have guessed, it all starts with your mind and a thought. In the action scene, the thought might be: *I'm going to kick this guy's ass!* In the drama scene, it could be: *I can't believe I just lost my best friend.*

When you have a thought, the brain releases a chemical associated with it. This chemical goes into the body, and the body generates a feeling based on that chemical.

It doesn't matter what caused the creation of the chemical. It could be an inner thought or from your external environment. It's like thinking about a tiger in front of you versus there actually being a tiger in front of you.

If you think about it hard enough, you can evoke the same feeling of fear you feel when there is a tiger in the room with you. The body doesn't know the difference!

That's how powerful your mind is.

Now, because we can give other people thoughts, then technically, we can make them feel whatever we want them to feel.

After they have the thought, they feel the feeling; then they take an action based on that feeling. So, if we're making people think things, and we make them feel things, then we can make them do things. We could say we're creating their reality.

There is a lot of power in this, and a lot of responsibility.

How will you use these powers?

Part 2 – Video for Business

Awareness

In my video production business, I use the consumer journey as my guide and apply video during each stage. This journey always starts with awareness. Someone must know your product or service exists before they can buy it, plain and simple.

We can use video to raise awareness on social media as video posts, stories, reels, shorts, or live streams. We can send direct video messages to thank someone for following our Facebook page or Instagram account. We can also send direct video messages to people who connect with us on LinkedIn. We could even pay for online video ads or TV commercials.

Regardless of how you raise awareness with video, there should always be a clear and simple call to action: Learn more.

In my business, I use these awareness videos to send people to my website. I'm never looking to close a deal here.

Consideration

In this stage, the potential customer is trying to decide whether your product or service is a good fit for them. They're looking for more information, they're doing some research, and usually end up on your website.

This is where you should have a *consideration* video. This video briefly explains who you are, what you do, how you do it, and who you work with, in about two minutes.

I like to front-end load these videos with as much value as possible to keep the viewer interested. This video acts like a natural filter, so by the end, the viewer will know for sure if you are the right fit for them.

Ideally, we want people to be a "yes," so they buy our product or service. However, it is okay for them to be a "no!"

In fact, I will argue it's a good thing if someone is a no. It's better to find out now before you're locked into a contract working with someone you can't stand!

The consideration video naturally filters out those who don't align with you. Instead, it connects you with your ideal clients. Aren't these the people you want to work with anyway?

Just like awareness videos, the consideration video needs a call to action. This time, it's a little more specific, based on your business and funnel. What do you need them to do to start working with you?

My current consideration video call to action is "Fill out the form below this video." The form submission goes to my email; then, I follow up to schedule a discovery call.

My next call to action (to make the process even easier) will be, "Click the button below to schedule a discovery call." Then, I simply show up to the meetings on my calendar, knowing it's with a person likely ready to get to work.

Purchase and Service

These are the next two stages of the consumer journey. You can use videos during these stages, for example, as explainer or training videos. Perhaps you have a product or service that isn't so easy to understand. Or maybe your product is a pre-recorded video course! You can also send a "thank you for your purchase" video.

Retention

This is the final stage, and it's all about keeping your customers coming back. This is where personalized thank-you videos and testimonials come in handy. Send these out five to seven times per year via email to show your appreciation and to share other customers' experiences. Who knows, maybe you get a testimonial validating a service someone didn't know you offered. Poof! They're back in the awareness stage, now interested in this new offer you have.

Part 3 – Creating Your Script Outline

Time to create something together! Yes, right now! Grab a pen and paper or open a Word document, and let's get started.

I'm going to give you a series of prompts that will become the script for your consideration video. This script does not have to be a word-for-word narrative. It can be as simple as an outline.

In fact, when delivering content on camera, I prefer speaking from the heart as opposed to reading off a teleprompter. These prompts help to plant the seeds of what you're going to say. So, when you're in front of a camera, you'll deliver your message in a way that feels more natural and authentic to the viewer.

Prompt 1 – What is the goal of this video?

We know this is a consideration video, but what do you want to achieve with this video? What is the purpose? Why are you even making this to begin with?

Prompt 2 – Who are you speaking to?

Who is your target audience? Hint: This is your ideal client. Take some time to think about your favorite clients, the ones that are just easy to work with. They always pay on time, you get along well, you could be friends outside of work, you just love them! This will be your audience because we want to attract more of them, right?

Prompt 3 – What's the message?

What are we trying to convey to these ideal clients? What do we want them to know after watching this video? What are the key takeaways?

Prompt 4 – Why is this important to them?

What value are they going to get out of working with you? What is it worth to them? What problem are you solving for them?

Prompt 5 – What do you want them to do after watching this video?

Are they calling a phone number? Clicking on a link? Registering for an event? Sending you an e-mail or a text? Filling out a form? This is your call to action. Consider how you want them to feel after watching this video. Remember, feelings drive the action.

Prompt 6 – What images come to mind when you imagine this video?

Are we inside or outside? In the office or at someone's home? Are we out in nature, maybe at a park? Or are we in the middle of a loud, bustling city? There are no wrong answers here. What colors do you see? Is there a particular style you have in mind? Is it slow, calm, and peaceful? Or is it fast-paced and energetic?

Prompt 7 – What sounds do you hear?

Do you hear music? If so, what is the style? The genre? The vibe? The pace? Do you hear sound effects? Are there birds chirping? Is there wind blowing through leaves on a tree? Do you hear cars and crowds of people? Again, there are no wrong answers.

Prompt 8 – What feelings do you have about this video?

What vibe do you want to bring to your viewers? Is it you on the video screen? Or do you have a spokesperson? How do you want this person to be seen?

Congratulations, you now have a script!

Once you've answered all these questions, you should review what you've written and add or subtract your answers as needed. At this point, you can take this to a video professional or pick up your own camera and start recording!

If you're going the DIY route, professional and pro-consumer cameras are widely available. And don't forget about your phone! These days, most phones are quite capable of capturing high-quality video.

Whether using your phone or a larger camera, I suggest using a tripod to keep your shot stable. Make sure you have plenty of good light so we can see your face clearly, and don't forget about audio. There are plenty of affordable microphones available online. Feel free to reach out if you need any recommendations on any of this equipment.

As you record, don't be afraid to mess up. Have fun with it! Remember, you can always edit out the bloopers. Or better yet, save them for a funny social media post.

After recording, you'll need to edit and add the music or sound effects you imagined. There are plenty of free and paid options when it comes to video editing software.

Free options include iMovie, Adobe Express, Canva, and Movavi. I'm sure there are others if you're up for a little online research. Alternatively, you can go to websites like Fiverr or Upwork to find very affordable video editors. Or check out your local university for a video editing intern!

Conclusion

You have the power to create reality for yourself and for others. The thoughts you create directly correspond to emotions in your body, which drive the actions taken in daily life.

The more awareness you bring to your thoughts, the more power you gain over your ability to create reality. The only question is, do you want a reality based on love or fear?

I know which one I'm choosing.

Love! Love! Love!

Kyle Steinle founded Do Good Video Productions, LLC in 2018 with a passion for video production and a newfound purpose in life to simply "do good." He holds a Bachelor of Science in Electronic Media and Film from Towson University and a Master of Science in Analytics and Knowledge Management from Notre Dame of Maryland University. As Owner and Executive Producer, his hope is to indirectly and positively serve the lives of individuals and local communities in need. He achieves this by providing video production services to small business owners in the health and wellness space, as well as to nonprofit organizations positively impacting local communities. Kyle is dedicated to operating Do Good Video with a harmonious balance of logical mind and open heart.

Outside of work, Kyle loves spending time in nature hiking and camping, exploring major mountain ranges on his snowboard, relaxing at the beach with his family, and watching movies with his wife.

Connect with Kyle:

Website: https://dogoodvideo.com/
Facebook: https://www.facebook.com/dogoodvideo
Instagram: https://www.instagram.com/dogoodvideo/
YouTube: https://www.youtube.com/@dogoodvideo
Vimeo: https://vimeo.com/dogoodvideo
LinkedIn: https://www.linkedin.com/in/kyle-steinle/
LinkedIn: https://www.linkedin.com/company/do-good-video-productions-llc

Chapter 19

Speak with SPARK

Strategies to Prepare, Practice, and Present Impactful Presentations

Meridith Grundei, Public Speaking and Presentations Skills Coach

> *I believe that you can change lives and save the world by telling your story, so what are you waiting for?*

My Story

My father had PTSD that surfaced when I was 11, a condition caused by exposure to Agent Orange that required surgery. The anesthesia triggered flashbacks 13 years after his final tour as a Marine in Vietnam.

"Don't upset your father!" my mother would often say. "He had a long day at work, so when he gets home, please don't argue with him." I was a budding teenager, and arguing was my jam. I was strong-willed and curious, so the response, "Because I said so," was never good enough for me.

Sadly, things escalated at home. My father became more verbally aggressive and, occasionally, physically aggressive. Mostly, he harmed himself by punching holes in the drywall or smashing a sprinkler against the brick house in frustration. Only once was he physical with me, but it was the verbal abuse that cut to my core. When my grades were subpar, he once called me a "piece of shit that didn't know anything." When my grades didn't improve, he took me out of the one thing I loved the most—dance. Naturally, this didn't help my grades. Instead, I rebelled more. Even though I was a good kid, I stopped going to class and ended up with a 1.2 GPA in my sophomore year of high school. A year later, when a therapist advised them to put me back into dance and give me more agency, it was too late. My peers improved, and I felt like I wasn't good anymore. My confidence was shaken to the core, and I felt less than.

When I was finally back in dance classes, I participated in the end-of-semester recital. For one of the dances, the choreographer said, "I want you all to come up with a line of text about what you want to be when you grow up, and you'll say it out loud from the stage."

"When I grow up, I want to be just like Wonder Woman!" were the first words I chose to shout from the stage. After the performance, the dance instructor approached me with a smile on her face and exclaimed, "You have a wonderful stage voice. You should take acting classes!"

I don't know how I convinced my parents or got into that classroom with six other eager students and my teacher, Maury Evans. There I was in my first-ever acting class, and her words changed my life forever!

As a younger kid, I was fairly shy. I cared way too much about what people thought of me and never felt like I fit in. No matter how many pairs of Guess jeans I convinced my mom to buy me—even though they were always too big because I could only shop from the sales rack—and no matter how big my friendship pin collection was, fitting in with the "popular" kids never seemed to work. It also didn't help that I was terrified to speak up in class, so I always hid in the back row in hopes that the teacher wouldn't call on me.

Sixth grade was going to suck if I sounded stupid or didn't know the answer, so it was easier to not say anything at all. This is probably why I gravitated to dance—because I didn't have to say anything—or so I thought.

Theater saved my life. It gave me the tools to start sharing my voice. It gave me someone else's words, the script, and characters from all walks of life to hide behind as I slowly started to find myself again.

My passion for performance continued through college and into the real world, when, after a stop in San Francisco, I stayed for four years doing experimental theater and sketch comedy. Doing sketch inspired me to move to Chicago, Illinois, to study improv at iO, the home of the long-form favorite, The Harold. It was through improv that I really found my voice because there was no longer a script. It was all my point of view. And yes, sometimes I played wacky characters, but these characters all emerged from me and my experiences. It was transformational. Not only did I start sharing my voice more, but I also became a better listener, performer, and human.

I also loved teaching it! I was already teaching theater games to kids in after-school programs: one I founded called Theater Monkey and several others throughout the city. For one of the programs I worked for, I co-facilitated a class with a core faculty member of The Second City, who recommended me for a job helping them create a curriculum for their youth program! I, of course, said, "Yes!" and there I was, teaching for the infamous Second City in Chicago. I did this for about four years, teaching all ages and occasionally co-facilitating workshops for their corporate division, which was called BizCo.

From here, I started finding my way into more rooms with business professionals. My first coaching client as a speaker coach was an executive with True Value Hardware in 2007. He shared the big stage with the CEO for their annual conference in Salt Lake City, Utah.

The more presentations I watched and the more I coached, the more I noticed that everyone sounded the same. All of the presentations, whether from middle management or senior leadership, had a similar cadence and energy.

I would sit in the audience and think to myself, "Is the audience getting any value from this? Are organizations losing potential opportunities because the audience doesn't clearly understand or remember their content?"

In good storytelling, there's an element of surprise. This is what keeps us hooked. In most presentations, this element of surprise, the story, or the emotional connection is often missing. Instead, most presentations are more focused on the what and not enough on the how or the why.

Frances Frei and her partner, Anne Morriss, are thought leaders and experts at how to fix, grow, and lead companies. If leadership is your jam, then look them up! Frances Frei gave a TED Talk several years ago that grabbed my attention. She talked about what she called the Triangle of Trust. The essence of the talk was that in order to build trust as a leader, you must have these three things: empathy, authenticity, and logic. The argument is that when trust is lost, it can almost always be traced back to a breakdown in one of these elements (Harvard Business Review, "Begin with Trust: The First Step to Becoming a Genuinely Empowering Leader" by Frances X. Frei and Anne Morriss).

This is true in presenting as well. Empathy, authenticity, and logic are needed in order to build trust with your audience, and more often than not, presenters are really good at sharing logic but not as intentional as they could be about finding empathy and bringing their true spirits and personalities forward.

In order for your diverse audiences with diverse ways of learning and retaining information to receive value, there needs to be more intentionality put into how we communicate our products, services, and ideas. This means we need clean visuals, more intentional messaging, and more ways to engage our audiences so they're not just listening to talking heads all day.

My mission is to transform how you present and give you the tools to better engage with your audiences so that when they leave the convention hall or conference room, your service, product, or inspired call to action is retained and remembered.

So what does this look like?

The Strategy

There are elements you need to consider if you want your audience to remember your product, idea, or services. And there's a simple structure that will help, including solutions for how to think about your visuals and ideas for how to practice more effectively.

Your Presentation Blueprint: Follow the below structure, step-by-step, if you want the most success with your talk:

PART ONE: Preparation

1. **Know your audience**
   Before you even think about your presentation and content, think about your audience. What do they know? What don't they know, and what do they need to know? Yes, they may be similar to the last audience you presented to, but each audience is unique. I work with a lot of engineers and designers who often forget that they can't deliver the same presentation they gave to fellow tech experts, customers, and stakeholders. These audiences have different needs. Your experts clearly understand your jargon and train of thinking, whereas your customers and stakeholders need you to simplify and translate. They need you to solve their problem.

2. **What is your objective/ End in mind**
   What do you want your audience to remember at the end of your talk? What is the purpose of your presentation?

3. **What are the key takeaways?**
   Most people can only retain up to three key points. What are the three takeaways that will lead your audience to your end in mind? Be specific.

Now that you're clear about who you're speaking to and the purpose of your presentation, let's work on your introduction.

PART TWO: Your Introduction

The introduction is my favorite part because beginnings matter, and those first few seconds count. Most people start their presentations with a salutation like, "Hi," "Thank you for having me, I'm so happy to be here. My name is. . ." and so on. Here's the thing—no one cares. Your audience wants you to solve their problem. Get creative and start there first! Get them engaged from the top. I imagine this will feel a little uncomfortable at first, but once you practice it a few times and bravely start this way in front of your audience, it will truly set you apart from other presenters:

1. **Your introduction structure:**

   - Your hook: This could be a story, an open-ended question, an anecdote, a quote, a startling statistic, etc. Think about what will grab their attention.

   - Who you are for credibility: Keep it brief. Please don't give us your resume and numerous awards.

   - The problem.

   - The solution, stating your key takeaways: What is your audience going to gain from your presentation?

   Here is an example:

Hook:

Did you know that according to a study done by The Harvard Business Review, 84% of business executives believe that effective presentations are critical to business success and can make a significant impact on the outcome of business deals?

Credibility:

My name is Meridith, and I'm a passionate nerd about helping you be a better speaker. I've been coaching leaders and their teams in technical fields for over a decade. I'm a former teacher of The Second City, and you can find me in a commercial or two playing an overly concerned mother.

Problem:

Today, let's talk about how you're losing potential customers because they don't clearly understand your products and services.

Solution:

My goal for you by the end of this presentation is to make sure you have new tools and a simple structure so your presentations feel not only effortless to prepare but, more importantly, that they're memorable. I'll do this by sharing how to better prepare, how to create an unforgettable introduction, and how to properly practice so that you're integrating the information and available to engage with your audience.

PART THREE: Your Conclusion and Call to Action (CTA)

For your conclusion, tie it back to the introduction, re-summarize the key takeaways, or tie it back to the story you shared. Make sure you clearly re-summarize the purpose of the presentation.

And finally, your call to action: What is it you want your audience to do? Are you inspiring them to take action? Then what is that action step? Do you need them to scan a QR code to get on your mailing list? Do you need them to fill out an evaluation?

Whatever it is, keep it simple, and do not overwhelm your audience with too many calls to actions. When you do this, you risk them doing nothing at all.

PART FOUR: Your Visuals

Visuals can be your slides, a prop, a video, or anything to best enhance and support your message. But before you dive into that PowerPoint, please ask yourself, "Do I need visuals, and if so, which ones will best support my message, if any at all?"

PART FIVE: Putting It All Together

Now that you have clearly thought out your presentation, let's put it all together:

- Your introduction
- Key takeaway #1
- Key takeaway #2
- Key takeaway #3
- Conclusion
- Call to action (CTA)

Practice Makes Prepared!

Now that you have your structure, it is time to practice! During my years of coaching people in presentation skills, I find a lot of people don't know how to practice in a helpful way. Here are a few ideas. And here's the deal—no one needs you to be perfect. Perfectionism is overrated. What they do need from you, however, is to understand the information enough so you can engage with them. This means that you have practiced enough to where you have not necessarily memorized your material, but you have integrated it.

Here we go:

- **Always practice out loud! Always.** Sitting at your computer and skimming the content won't get you to where you need to be.

Instead, stand up and say the words out loud. Engage your entire body.

- **Visualize yourself in front of your audience.** Stand in the middle of your room, living room, or conference room. Imagine where your audience is and talk to them. Visualize yourself connecting with them and doing a great job!

- **Chunk it out.** What's the saying? Don't eat the entire elephant? Take small portions of your talk and practice. For example, most 20-minute presentations, if written out, are about eight to ten pages in length. Try practicing the first five pages or five minutes of your presentation in repetition for 20-30 minutes, and then take a five to ten-minute break. Go outside for fresh air, grab a snack, or return a few emails, but take a break. Then come back and review those five pages or five minutes and then move on to pages six to ten, practice, take a break, and repeat.

- **Use visuals or images.** I had one client who needed to memorize her talk and had a hard time remembering the order of things, so I suggested that she find an image that represented each paragraph or section of her speech. So in the left-hand margins, you saw an image of Superman followed by the Eiffel Tower, followed by a plumber's wrench, etc. These visuals helped her recognize what was next on paper and in her head.

There are several techniques you can use to help you memorize or integrate the material, but whatever works for you, please remember that the more you practice, the more confident you'll feel.

Whether you're just starting your speaking journey or you've been doing this for a while, I hope you picked up a few nuggets of wisdom here. I know we can change the world by sharing our stories. Even if you feel like stories should be secondary in your profession, I challenge you—they need to be primary. Because at the end of every product or service, no matter how technical, there's a person and an opportunity for connection. Make it count.

Meridith Grundei is a creative doer, mom, and entrepreneur. She leads workshops and delivers talks globally as a public speaking and presentation consultant and coach for some prominent industry and educational institutions such as Amazon AWS, Panasonic, Pfizer, Merck, Stanford University, Mercer, and the CU Leeds School of Business. Some of her private clients are conscious CEOs and leaders from organizations like Google, BKV Corporation, Edward Jones, and Integrated Partners, to name a few. People who work with Meridith are guaranteed results with a whole lot of serious fun!

Connect with Meridith:

LinkedIn: https://www.linkedin.com/in/meridith/

TikTok for presentation tips: https://www.tiktok.com/@grundeicoaching

The Grundei Coaching website: https://www.grundeicoaching.com/

Part 3
Staying Power
(A Smarter Long Game)

Chapter 20

Lifelong Learning
The Key to Business Growth and Evolution
DeeAnna Merz Nagel, D.Th, LMHC

> *Go ahead! Go for it! Take that basketweaving course. It counts!*

My Story

"You should teach a course for us here at the Institute."

"But I'm not a coach!"

"Then become one."

That's crazy. I'm a psychotherapist. What? I'm just gonna become a coach now? For what? So I can teach one course?

And so it began. I stepped into lifelong learning, and I haven't looked back.

It was the late 2000s, and up to that point, I spent most of my career working in traditional mental health agencies and private practice. I had a penchant for teaching, and I was a big fan of online therapy long before it was a thing. I traveled the states teaching continuing education and professional development courses to other therapists who wanted to learn how to incorporate technology into their practice with clients.

It wasn't the sexiest of topics, but I was determined to enlighten people on the benefits of technology-delivered psychotherapy. After all, this was breaking barriers to accessibility, and it was the new frontier. All my efforts were about pushing that agenda—the next article, speaking engagement, or course I took—it was all about furthering my knowledge and expanding the landscape regarding the incorporation of technology into the counseling profession. This task force, that ethics committee—I could go on and on.

"Would you be willing to be a guest for our monthly call?"

I would speak to coaching faculty and students about keeping communications confidential via phone, chat, and email using encryption.

Okay. This is a tad out of my wheelhouse. Life coach? Executive coach? Wellness coach? I guess encryption is encryption whether one is a therapist or a coach. Still, it feels like a stretch.

I decided to stretch. The school had a record number of participants on the call, and with the warm reception I received, I was asked if I would like to teach a course on online coaching.

While coaches and therapists have overlapping skills and scopes of practice, the two have distinct differences. For starters, coaching is not regulated. Counseling is.

In my initial discussion with the Dean of Students, I explained, "I don't feel prepared to take on this opportunity because, well, *I'm not a coach.*" She encouraged me to get coach training to ease my angst about not feeling qualified to teach a course for coaches. "You can become a Board

Certified Coach (BCC) with just 30 hours of training since you already have a Master's degree in counseling."

*Do I **really** want to do this? I mean, that's 30 hours of my life I won't get back and it kinda takes me off my path.*

Little did I know that this offer to overcome imposter syndrome, preparing me to teach one course on a similar topic to a similar audience, would shift my mindset and change my trajectory. I obtained 30 hours of coach training, allowing me to sit for the test and become credentialed as a coach.

There. I'm prepared now. I can do this, and nobody will question my authority on the topic. Whew.

Within a few years, I curated and facilitated several online, self-directed coach courses for the Institute, all steeped in coach competency and ethics.

Alongside my new-found place in the coaching world, I struggled personally with health issues and a bad marriage; I knew I wasn't alone. Many of us do that— juggling the personal while propping up our professional lives. But something had to give. I was unwell and in dis-ease.

I struggled with lymphedema (born with it) and an acquired autoimmune disorder (sarcoidosis), which was triggered by exposure to black mold. Every time I had one symptom under control, another popped up. It was like Whack-a-Mole. I thought I was holistic with my approach to my health but something kept nudging me to step up my game. I just didn't know what that meant. But I was very mindful about paying attention to what would show up. Time and time again, a new holistic approach would cross my path by way of a book, a class, a colleague- so much so that I could not ignore the signs. And my marriage—just please—I was so ready to be done. But I didn't know where the exit ramp was. Again, all I knew was to pay attention. Of course, it was a balancing act while I kept my foot on the gas with my professional life. At the same time, I managed that next medical appointment and squeezed in my own therapy while making a last-ditch effort to save my marriage through couple's counseling—even though I knew that if it was last-ditch, the saving wouldn't happen.

Keep in mind that up to this point, I conceptualized lifelong learning as something required of me. After all, as a psychotherapist and now a coach, I was required to obtain so many continuing education hours each year.

Imagine this mindset as I walked out of my latest of many appointments—this one, a dermatologist—got in my car, stared into space, thinking, *what's next?* And like a neon sign, I received a message—an intuitive download: *Take a Reiki course. Now. Do it. Take an online Reiki course.*

Reiki? Do I even know what Reiki is? Some sort of energy something-or-other? What? Really?

I followed that download and enrolled in my first adult learning course, which had nothing to do with obtaining a degree, license, or certification or maintaining them. I took a course for my own self-care—for me, just me—and it grew me in big ways.

During that time, I was introduced to essential oils. I bought a starter kit. I diffused, sniffed, and applied essential oils every day in every way. The oils shifted me. Reiki shifted me. My work slowly shifted, too, and my marriage was something to finally address—upheaval, up-leveling, upended!

This feels a bit unsettling, yet like coming home all at the same time. How can it be? I don't know where this step is going to lead, but here I go!

I kept following the path. My health improved, I knew my marriage was done, and I was empowered to take the next steps. The next thing you know, I declared myself *an intuitive*, not just 'intuitive.' I pronounced myself out of the pixie closet.

When I first came out of the intuitive closet, I received several not-so-nice, crinkled-nose, nasty-gram emails and comments from skeptics. I was a bit surprised at the un-boundaried responses from fellow licensed mental health professionals who apparently didn't approve, as evidenced by comments such as "Seriously?" and "WTF?" I was told, "You're committing professional suicide," but I just kept following my gut and inner voice.

I took an aromatherapy course just because I wanted to learn about oils and the science behind the healing benefits. I took courses on Spirit guides, chakra balancing and akashic records. I discovered Tarot and oracle cards and attended a three-day in-person workshop on manifesting. I was learning. I had fun. And I was reaping the benefits of a life with intention.

And guess what? It all showed up in my work. I went from a straight-laced, in-the-box therapist teaching ethics and legal implications about delivering therapy online to teaching Reiki, alternative practices, chakra healing, and more.

My personal endeavors dovetailed with my professional endeavors in ways that expanded me beyond what I could've imagined. I never considered that my own personal growth—my personal, out-of-the-box interests—could have such a positive impact on my career.

Now, I'm a mentor and consultant for many therapists and coaches who want to discover new ways to work and serve their clients. I'm the person who has stretched the boundaries and discovered a new meaning to "scope of practice." Now, I'm the one who tells the psychologist, "Yes, you can utilize a Tarot or oracle deck in your work with others. It's a projective technique. Let me teach you. Let's start with Carl Jung."

The Strategy

My story may not be an obvious match to yours. You might be a web developer or a veterinarian. A closer look though, and we might discover a vibrational match. You're reading this book. My guess—you're a lightworker.

A lightworker is someone who desires to share a higher level of consciousness and light into the world. Lightworkers may be in the direct helping professions, but lightworkers may also be working in many different vocations. A lightworker is the postal worker who delivers your mail with a smile, the grocery store clerk who always has a pleasant demeanor, the physician who always takes time to listen. Lightworkers show up in different skins.

If you identify as a lightworker, you might know that you have to keep your light shining to be a beacon for others. That light can only shine bright if you keep the lens clean and clear. Think about a lighthouse. Those large fresnal lenses come with an entire protocol to keep the lighthouse shining bright. Our body is the lighthouse housing the fresnal lens.

It makes sense that if you want your business to grow, you must grow personally. That's where holistic lifelong learning comes in. Don't just learn to check a box or gain another credential. Learn because you're hungry for knowledge. Your soul wants you to learn.

You might see a course online, a class at a local college, or a lecture at the local library that's perhaps on a topic completely different from your professional work. In fact, it might be far removed from anything you do or how you identify. If your gut stirs, go for it! Take the leap because you never know where it'll show up next in your personal or professional (or both) life.

Here are some examples.

The team manager at a tech company decided to take a coach training course because deep down inside, there was always a desire to be a life coach. Courses completed, credential in-hand, this team manager has an entirely new set of tools to utilize at work and decides to stay as a team manager because the coach training enhanced communication and team-building skills. The team manager discovers he is right where he wants to be.

The occupational therapist, who is required to take continuing education courses and is given a stipend from the school board, opts to spend her own money on a chakra balancing course. And it doesn't count toward her required hours. She has no idea what the course will do for her, but she was drawn to the course and decided to go for it. Maybe she'll consider a career shift. Maybe she'll start a side gig. And maybe she'll become more balanced herself so she can be more present and shine for the students she serves.

The architect who's on the top of her game but burning out, running her own company, and juggling family life in the midst decides to spend two days at a spa retreat to unwind and become centered again. She arrives at this beautifully appointed place and immediately feels calm. In conversation she discovers the owner of the retreat also teaches Feng Shui. The architect's interest is piqued. She decides to attend the next Feng Shui workshop, and an entirely new energetic perspective, along with accompanying tools, is introduced to her professional and personal life.

These examples provide just a glimpse into another dimension that opens up when we pay attention to opportunities and listen with our full senses—the sixth sense and our third ear. What may not seem like a fit may be just the fix we need.

Oh wow! Look, Honey! The local community college is offering a course on basket weaving! I have always been curious about that.

Go for it! To quote Dr. Suess, "Oh, the places you'll go!"

Dr. DeeAnna Merz Nagel is a seasoned psychotherapist, clinical supervisor, coach, and aromatherapist. Her work is deeply influenced by an intuitive perspective, with teaching being the core aspect of her current endeavors. With over 30 years of experience in direct service to individuals, families, and groups, she is now solely and soulfully dedicated to facilitating learning in the healing arts and sharing insights from her own direct experiences. She guides practitioners on clinical, psycho-spiritual, and intuitive learning journeys!

DeeAnna's aspiration is to guide individuals as they learn to guide others, whether it be as therapists, coaches, energy healers, or intuitive practitioners. She is eager to help practitioners incorporate alternative approaches into their practice. She aims to serve as a gatekeeper to the counseling profession by providing skilled and synergistic clinical supervision training and helping practitioners integrate metaphysical, psycho-spiritual, and subtle energy methods into their client work. She creates professional development experiences that seamlessly align with personal growth.

DeeAnna has also created Essential Soul Care®, a psycho-spiritual model featuring a course, a book, and an oracle deck. She has authored several other books, book chapters, and articles. Her work has garnered recognition in national publications such as the *New York Times*, *USA Today*, and *Women's Health*.

Beyond her professional identity, DeeAnna is a devoted cat mother, a friend to many, and an admirer of beautiful things like doilies, fine bone china, and Victorian lamps. Her surroundings reflect her love for Byzantine art, flamingos, and crystals. And, of course, she incorporates essential oils into her moon rituals, too!

Connect with DeeAnna:

Website:
https://deeannamerznagel.com

https://deeannamerznagel.com/links

https://deeannamerznagel.com/books

Instagram and X: @deeannanagel

Chapter 21

When Your Business is Stuck
A Results Strategy to Achieve Flow and Success—Again
Frank Byrum

> *Despite careful planning, projects frequently take twice as long and cost twice as much as anticipated, with course corrections and a bit of luck still essential for success.*

My Story

Argh!

I screamed in pain, followed by a string of expletives, I'm told, although I don't recall either the scream or the following cursing.

Fainting often follows intense pain.

Why am I on the floor?

To my right, an overturned richly grained reddish-brown teak stool.

The semi-squared corner of the white-tiled jacuzzi was inches from my head.

I strained to look up through my watering eyes at the aluminum edge of the glass shower door.

My left ankle pounded like a bass drum. Woozy and dripping, I was on all fours, deep crimson dots reflecting the harsh incandescence.

Why is there blood on the floor?

Time blurred; I tried to focus. *Ugh,* through a throbbing migraine.

Have you ever woken in a throbbing haze, trying to piece together what went wrong? It's much like waking up to a broken project—the confusion can be overwhelming.

Trying to remember all the events up to the moment can be exhausting and leave you feeling hopeless.

How did it come to this? You may ask. The more you focus, the deeper the impenetrable fog bank—waves of memories, vignettes, chronologically disordered.

So many decisions and actions are done correctly. You toiled, did your homework, paid the proverbial dues, found a niche, a wedge into the market, a gap others missed, ripe for disruption and leverage.

Crawled. I crawled here.

Rivulets streamed down my brow, another drop of blood. *I'm going to be sick; I'm going to throw up. I'm going to throw…*

All the hard work, the hours, the investment, and it isn't working.

> Eureka instant,
> A torrent of ideas flow,
> Pitches, proposal.

You can feel the pain deep in your gut; you can't say it. It's a jinx to admit—*it isn't working.*

Ever hold out too long, running so hard, rarely feeling a full, deep belly breath?

A flush and flurry of an initial engagement, then the slowly coming second.

So close, I can feel it.

Just keep believing. New projects can break, and it feels something like a broken leg.

It's just a bad sprain.

My mentor once told me, "It takes twice as long as it takes." On another occasion he added, "and twice as much money."

Nowadays, in his later 70s, he is Chairman after recently passing the baton to a newly-minted CEO.

Recently, he refactored, "And a bit of luck." Business is as inseparable as his skin.

"It's in his blood," as is oft said.

Initially, unconsciously, then consciously, I realized I was rubbing the side of my brow.

Using both hands to sit up, blood rivers trickle down my arm.

More expletives.

"What the?"

Blushingly, scanning her mahogany eyes for answers: *I blacked out?*

"I'm calling 911," Maria's opening volley.

Attempting an appeal to her frugality, "It's too expensive, it's just a bad sprain—"

"Hello, yes, my husband just passed out…"

"—I'll go to the ER in the morning."

With comical Italian American hand gestures, Remember *Three's Company* circa 1982, the slapstick sitcom? That is what happened next," forestalling the inevitable giggle.

"In slow motion, you sat straight up, and slowly your noggin plunked."

And Bam!

You thwacked the sink."

Tracing all my steps.

Stepped off the curb. Twisted my ankle. Caught myself with hands and knees. Vroom, car headlights. Oh shit! Executed backward roll.

Struggled to stand up.

Taking the checkered flag, racing heart winner, car loser.

"Are you okay?"

Struggling to see the shadow: *Blurred, slight build, silver-blonde, long-hair—70ish, maybe.*

"Yes, I'm fine. Thank you. I'm fine. Really, I'm fine."

Trembling, body thrusting to the moon to stand, both knees bleeding, throbbing, and busted.

Damn it! My best AG jeans! $245 bucks!

Proudly, I started walking, deciding on the beeline, through the park. First step—doubled over and heaved. Second step—a faltering stumble, then a limp. Backdoor light about a football field away.

Home. I can make it; I will be okay.

My gut says: I'm all right; it's just a really bad sprain.

My ego says: I've got this! I've been here before.

Who am I kidding?

Who are you kidding?

You know, beneath all the fear you've pushed down to get to this point, the effort is stalled, the market isn't responding. "Where are the customers?"

Another mentor once told me, "It's best to have a clear failure or clear success. It's the middle ground that's hard to navigate."

I sat in silence, replaying each step: *Did I throw up behind Cindi's?* Seconds pass.

"Mr. Byrum, what day is it? I'm Ray and this is Jason, and we are going to help you."

Wow, what just happened? I remember her calling 911 and talking and blank.

"Thursday."

Oh, likely 15-minutes. Three is not a charm: *Must have blacked-out again.*

"Can you tell me what happened?"

I snapped back, fully engaged, answered every question with scientific clarity and precision, and they still put me on the stretcher for the ignoble ride to the emergency room.

I've spent nearly 40 years in high-tech projects, products, and related research. Lived many times between startup and IPO. Never have I seen failure for pure technology reasons.

A friend was introduced as a "successful entrepreneur" as part of his bio for a conference. His first words after the introduction have always stayed with me: "I'm not a successful entrepreneur; I'm an entrepreneur who has had a success."

I feel the same. Overall, I've had many successes, and still find myself working for others in and out of season.

". . .we can't take him. He will have to go to a trauma unit…"

That woke me up again.

Actually. My wife calls me "actually-man." We passed five emergency rooms, but we made our way to the regional emergency trauma center.

For a sprain. Jeez.

"It's a bad sprain, right?" She blushed, eyes downturn, shaking her head, no.

"You will have to wait for the radiologist."

I'm not successful enough to retire—yet. I've found a niche in high-risk advanced technologies and related project turnarounds. That seems to be my skill set. I've helped many early entrepreneurs push past Death Valley and get their ideas to market.

And I've helped close down a start-up or two or three. I've also seen poor executive decisions, one particularly crushing—more than a $50-million evaluation with my investment and the second, lifetime billion-dollar opportunity.

Both, I believed to be my *coup de grâce*. I had dreams of becoming a regional venture capitalist or at the very least, a startup angel investor.

First-step programs start with an admission.

Admission is a form of awareness.

"It's broken."

Damn it!

Just like my left fibula, accepting the reality is a deeply difficult first step toward recovery.

Returning to my room, Maria with a police escort. "What?"

"It's broke," holding back the tears over the torture.

I was mostly silent through the CT scan and trauma-related diagnostics.

It appears that blacking out and hitting my head (and with my daily meds) is a serious matter, and there was a possibility of internal bleeding (in my brain).

Oh, *regional trauma center*. Thank you!

It was time to accept the evidence.

Is it time for you to accept the evidence?

Is it time for the three-As?

Step one—Awareness.

"Mr. Byrum, you have a broken left fibula. Just above the smaller bone in your left lower leg; it's just above your ankle."

"What does that mean?"

"We are sending you home in an air-cast, and I'm referring you to an orthopedic surgeon for follow-up. Would you like any medicine for your pain?"

It wasn't a sprain; I couldn't deny it any longer. All the pain, the X-rays, the doctor, it all aligned.

Step two—Alignment.

It's been 50 days since I broke my leg. For the first 30 days, I spent 23 hours a day in an air-cast with my leg propped above my heart and my MacBook Pro on my lap.

Even with all my denial, restlessness, and boredom, I've had to get in alignment with the recovery treatment.

So, it's time to admit your effort needs a drastic recovery, abandon what you have avoided; and it's time to align all your focus and resources towards recovery.

Step three—Abandon.

It's time to let go, abandon all the reasons you're using to put off the reality and move on to recovery. All the evidence is in alignment, there's no reason to ignore the truth any longer.

Recently, a friend paraphrased a Tony Robbins quote: "Success is related to the number of difficult discussions you are willing to have." And I would add—the hardest person to have an honest conversation with is—yourself.

The Strategy

Allocate at least two hours without any following planned activities. I recommend at least a 30-minute post-exercise buffer, specifically so that you can keep going if necessary. When initially starting, it's important not to be emotionally rushed by your next appointment.

Find the quietest place possible—in nature, a park, or a quiet room. Use noise-canceling headsets as a last resort.

This initial work will take several sessions; try not to feel rushed. Rushing to another task is an easy form of avoidance.

The initial goal is to get your thoughts on paper, and then you may need at least 24 hours before taking another look and refinement.

In my focus, I brew a small pot of tea, bring a pen and writing pad, and sit outside, away from distractions.

For this exercise, we're going to use the acrostic RECOVERY to get some clarity. Write the first things that come to mind for each;

in a later exercise, each of these will be edited, expanded, and curated. Don't worry about grammar, spelling, or proper sentences. At this point, consider yourself going through a self-directed brainstorming exercise.

RECOVERY STEPS

- Reassess objectives
- Evaluate failures
- Communicate openly
- Organize a plan
- Validate processes
- Empower the team
- Realign resources
- Yield improvements

Remember, this is a paper exercise. Turn off or store your computer and cell phone. No cheating, this will distract from your full attention to the initial recovery diagnosis.

Double check, no cellphone, right? No dings or alarms, right?

Take a deep breath, filling the lungs from the bottom to the top. Let out a slow, long sigh through your mouth. Repeat this process two additional times.

R—Reassess Objectives. It's important to be clear about your requirements. Often, this starts with a clear market need or problem statement, an ideal customer, and a specific benefit.

Offering a new idea to a preoccupied gruff colonel, he barked, "So what? Be specific. Be concise."

I propose you do the same; what is your: "So, what?" Why would anyone really care about your effort, project, product, or solution? Be as concise as possible, and try to make it understandable to someone who knows nothing about your technology or domain of expertise.

Are your goals relevant to your ideal customer and are they achievable in a reasonable amount of time, given you or your team's current capabilities and resourcing?

Are the market conditions right, or are you having to go to extremes to explain your effort?

What have you been telling your ideal customer? Are you having to explain non-standard definitions? Write down—need elevator pitch.

Take a deep breath, filling the lungs from the bottom to the top, and let out a slow, long sigh through your mouth. Do this again. And once again.

E—Evaluate Failures. This isn't about blame; it's about being precise with what isn't working.

If you can only think of blame, then get a separate piece of paper—a parking lot— and get that out of your headspace.

Here are a few prompts.

Concisely identify what's going wrong.

Do you have clear project management practices?

Did you allocate the right and enough resources?

Is there an external factor you didn't consider?

Stand up for a minute and stretch, refill your drink, or take a bio-break.

Start again. Take a deep breath, filling the lungs from the bottom to the top and let out a slow long sigh through your mouth. Do this again. And once again.

C—Communicate Openly. Your team looks to you as the leader, and even good leaders get caught up in ideas.

Did you foster an environment where your team could express concerns, their ideas, or give honest feedback?

Is there an unspoken penalty for disagreeing with you? One indicator may be that everyone agrees with you all the time.

Who on your team do you need to go back and listen to again?

Who on your team doesn't speak often? Go and chat with them. Be curious and ask questions.

What are the three things you really need to communicate to your team?

Remember, you set the tone for success. Write all this down for follow-up later.

I've often heard, "The boss listens first and speaks last."

O—Organize your plan. In as few notes as possible, identify a few steps to address the failures from your evaluation above. What will you do to avoid these in the future?

Are your milestones clear? What can you defer? Is there a requirement you are still trying to define?

It's time for another break. Take at least a ten-minute walk. Stretch again, refill your drink, or take a bio-break.

Start again. Take a deep breath, filling the lungs from the bottom to the top, and let out a slow, long sigh through your mouth. Do this again. And once again.

V—Validate Processes. Do you need new methodologies, tools, or software? Or are your requirements too overbearing and so detailed as to stifle any creativity or variation?

Do you need a brainstorming session? Or does your team need one without you?

Do you need more customer use cases or usage scenarios?

E—Empower the Team. Have you invested in the right level of training for your team? Do you allow your team to operate and make decisions or does every decision get cleared by the boss?

Do you recognize the individual and unique strengths each team member brings?

Is there a member who needs help and isn't keeping up? Who seems lost more than not?

Is there a poisonous element sucking energy from an otherwise productive group?

R—Realign Resources. This includes all resources—people and material resources. At times, this means delaying a resource to help the team focus or maybe engaging an outside resource to bring in domain expertise or help work through the details of all the steps in this process.

Y—Yield Improvements. It's important to monitor what you're changing and implementing above.

How will you monitor progress?

What are your metrics?

Be careful what you measure; poor metrics may lead to undesirable team behaviors.

Continual improvement—you will want to continually review your plans and initially maybe monthly and revise accordingly. The goal is to make tactical changes, not knee-jerk reactions that will cause confusion and chaos in the team.

Ultimately, you will want to assess the gains/losses at least monthly.

Now, put this away for at least 24 hours. On day two, read through without stopping. Next, get a red pen or marker and make edits, corrections, or additions.

Give yourself a few more rounds of this exercise until you are satisfied that you have captured all the essentials.

There are many next steps possible: overview the key takeaways with a mentor or close adviser, review with your team lead, develop a communication plan, expand and detail your plan, and so forth.

For additional resources, connect below or send me an email.

Frank Byrum is a scientist, technologist, and best-selling author who has spent the last four decades on a spiritual journey, the last few of which have been focused on deep self-healing. He is an entrepreneur who has had several successes and currently serves as Vice-President of Innovation for a high-tech endeavor, managing as well as contributing to several advanced technology and artificial intelligence projects. He serves on several technology advisory boards and as a consultant to several companies; and serves as a mentor to many.

Frank blends his technical expertise with a deep inner journey of self-discovery. His crisis of faith led to decades of searching various wisdom traditions and teachers, grounded in the simple truth of Mathew 7:7—*"Ask, and it shall be given you; seek, and ye shall find; knock, and it shall be opened unto you"* (KJV).

For years, he has shared his understanding with friends, family, students, and associates as he continued to research and practice. He earnestly believes everyone can benefit from the foundation of practical daily practice, and it's the best way to "be in the world, but not of the world."

He blends both the outer and inner work in his technologies and consulting endeavors.

Today, his daily practice includes tea, breath work, prayer and meditation, martial arts katas, Qi-Gong energy work, and wisdom studies. He resides in southeastern Virginia, where he practices, teaches, and writes.

Connect with Frank:

LinkedIn: https://www.linkedin.com/in/frankbyrum/
Website: https://quantumstack.tech
Email: frank@quantumstack.tech
Website: themindfulpathway.com
Email: frank@themindfulpathway.com
Twitter: https://twitter.com/MindfulPathway or @MindfulPathway
Instagram: https://www.instagram.com/tfbyrum

Chapter 22

Protect Your Empire
Legal Documents All Small Business Owners Need
Karen Hulme Alegi, Attorney

> You **are** your business. You need your personal estate planning documents in place to protect the empire you are about to build.

My Story

I was in my mid-30s and practicing law for about five years. I was an associate in a smaller law firm handling civil litigation, domestic matters, contract disputes, and small business counseling. As any service professional my age, I diligently "worked up the ladder" and busted my butt to impress the partners I worked for.

At this time, I believed success in my field meant being a partner in a private law firm. That's where the prestige is as an attorney and presumably the salary too! The career track often goes as follows: start at a law firm as an associate, move up to senior associate, then partner, and then equity partner. *Equity* means that you're also an owner of the firm in some percentage, along with your fellow equity partners, who are now your business partners.

Law firms are just businesses, LLCs, PAs, and PCs; only the owners must be licensed attorneys. While the structure varies greatly, it's often the case that to move up the ladder, someone at the top has to leave (die, retire, or quit). Since equity partner is the pinnacle of an attorney's career path, they rarely quit or retire.

So what did this mean for me? My firm was small—less than ten attorneys. There were two attorneys at the top of the firm. At the time, one of them was older than the typical retirement age, which means he definitely qualified for social security. In my eagerness to move up, I kept anticipating an announcement from the partnership. Anytime there was an unexpected meeting called or a social invite to the attorneys and spouses, I thought he'd make a retirement announcement. Over the course of a couple of years, that announcement never came. Then, one day, the number two attorney made the passing comment about number one, "He's not going anywhere anytime soon." Meaning he had no plans in the near future to retire. *Wait, what? Shit.*

Now how was I going to move up?

And how long would I have to wait for there to be room at the top?

What was I working so hard for?

My salary was okay, but not where I wanted it to be. And my pay didn't depend on how well I did my job or the amount of hours I put in week to week. Of course, I had billable hour goals, and my client's satisfaction was important. But when I achieved a great result, there was no merit bonus. I rarely even received a "nice job" or a pat on the back from management. Naturally, when discussing compensation, I was told that my pay would increase if I generated more work through my own marketing and networking efforts. Of course, I knew business generation was an important element of being a successful attorney in private practice. But after a couple of years, I thought: *Why am I doing this business generation for them?*

The firm wasn't mine. I wasn't an owner and apparently wouldn't be for quite a while. Even if I did become an equity partner, I'd have a small percentage in a business that would still be majority-managed by attorneys twice my age. We had very different ideas on business management, technology, staffing, and practice management. *Do I even want to own part of a business where I have little to no say in how it's run?*

By the end of that calendar year, I gave my notice. Thereafter, I formed a legal partnership and real estate company. I became a business owner and began to build my empire. I know what you're thinking: *Empire? Who does this lady think she is?* But the way I see it, if you don't see your business and finances as an empire, who else will? Empires don't happen overnight. Empires take time to build. You begin with little steps, good structures, and a vision. You'll make mistakes and learn a **lot** along the way. The fact that you're reading this book is an excellent beginning step! All of the chapters here will help you form your vision and take steps to lay your solid structures. Then build, build, build!

Personal matters are often neglected when you become a business owner. Often we're so focused *on* the business we forget we **are** the business. We have to have our own shit taken care of before the business can take off from our shoulders. Your personal estate planning is essential to protect your assets and control the management of your property.

The Strategy

Every adult should have at least basic estate planning documents in place. However, I often hear the following from folks who think they don't need planning.

"I don't have kids."

"My spouse just gets everything, right?"

"I don't have anything anyway."

"I'm single; why do I need estate planning?"

Although these issues vary a bit from state to state, the documents we'll discuss are necessary for everyone, regardless of marital status or family situation. As a business owner, you now have a very important asset to protect; your business!

Before we go further, it's important to note that the laws regarding estate planning documents are state-specific. Our discussion here will be about general processes and recommendations. Of course, you should consult with a local attorney in your area before taking action. I also never recommend using any do-it-yourself online legal websites. These documents are fraught with errors. It'll cost you much more if you get it wrong. Invest in getting assistance from a competent local attorney.

As a business owner, you will have important business relationships, own company property, be a party to contracts, and have bank accounts. All of these should be in the name of your business, but only *you* have the authority to act for your business. What would happen if you suddenly were unable to communicate or show up for work? Perhaps you're in an accident and taken to the hospital or suffer a stroke. Without the proper documents in place, there'll be no one with the authority to manage your business when you can't.

Financial Power of Attorney

The first document you should have in place is a financial power of attorney, also called a *durable* power of attorney. Any person over the age of 18 and mentally competent can sign a power of attorney giving another person, called an agent or attorney-in-fact, the authority to do anything and everything that the person could do with their property. This power only kicks in when you cannot manage your own affairs, and two medical professionals agree in writing. The person giving the power of attorney is called the *principal*. The authority in the document often includes the power to sell real estate, close or open bank accounts, and sign contracts in the name of the principal. These documents can be customized to address a limited number of assets or are very broad. The key component to the power is that all actions must be for the benefit of the principal, not the agent. So long as the agent acts in good faith, the agent does not bear any personal liability for the financial obligations of the principal.

When this power of attorney is executed and used properly, the agent can easily manage and maintain the principal's assets, accounts, and property and even talk to the bank, mortgage company, and any other person on the principal's behalf. Banks and other institutions cannot refuse to accept a power of attorney properly executed under the state law of the place it was signed.

Healthcare Power of Attorney

In addition to property and finances, you will need to give authority to another person to make medical decisions for you and be able to speak to your doctors when you're incapacitated. Under current federal and state laws, healthcare providers aren't permitted to discuss a person's health or medical information with anyone else unless they have that person's written authorization. This limitation equally applies to spouses and adult children. Once someone is already in the hospital or otherwise no longer able to communicate, that person can no longer sign an authorization to release information. You must have a healthcare power of attorney in place before you have any medical issues.

A healthcare power of attorney can include several provisions. At a minimum, it names an agent with whom your healthcare professionals are permitted to discuss your medical care, also called a HIPAA Waiver. This authorization typically lists a first choice and a backup and can also list "co-agents." For most situations, I rarely recommend co-agents on any power of attorney. I encourage my clients to pick the one person who is most able to make difficult decisions in stressful situations and name that person as the first choice. Only if your first choice is unavailable can your second choice agent be your decision maker. The purpose of naming one person at a time is to give certainty and clarity to your doctors, nurses, and other healthcare professionals when tough decisions must be made for you.

Your healthcare agent will be your treatment decision-maker once you can no longer communicate alone. Such treatment decisions can include whether or not to have surgery, consent to testing or transfusions, and end-of-life care options. This last piece is called an advance directive. This document was once referred to as a "living will," but that is a terrible misnomer and creates a lot of confusion. So we shall never use that phrase again! Advance directive language has been standardized throughout most states and will list three different end-of-life medical conditions. For each condition, the principal can select one of three treatment options. These range from letting natural death occur, with or without a feeding tube, to using all available medical means to extend life. These statements are then included in your healthcare power of attorney. The purpose is to give as much information about what you want to your decision-maker as possible when they have to make this decision on your behalf. You can imagine how difficult and stressful this situation will be. So you can help make this decision a bit less stressful by telling your agent what you want in advance.

As a business owner, you need to have these two powers of attorney in place at the beginning of your journey. You need to ensure the continuance of your business in the event something happens to your ability to run the business yourself.

Last Will and Testament

Are we really going to talk about death at the beginning of your empire-building? Isn't that a buzz kill? Well, yes, but let's get this very important matter resolved and off your plate so you can then continue forward and build your empire so you have something to pass on to your loved ones.

A Will is the document that says who your property goes to after you pass away. But it does more than that. Your Will designates a trusted person to manage your property after your death and take the steps necessary to transfer or liquidate your property and disburse the funds to your heirs. In Maryland, this person is called a Personal Representative (PR). Other states may call this person an Executor or Administrator. If you're married, it's common to name your spouse as your PR, but you're not required to. If unmarried, it's common to name a sibling or close friend. If you do not have a Will in place at the time of your death, state laws establish a priority order based on family relationships. This default list could very well cause an undesired result, depending on your family situation. That's why everyone needs to have a Will in place naming the person you choose to be in charge of your property.

A Will is important because it allows your designated PR to transfer your property faster, more efficiently, and less expensive than if someone has to take all these actions without a Will. It also avoids the confusion and frustration your loved ones will experience if you don't have a Will in place. I've worked with many clients who have had to figure out their deceased relative's matters without any authority or direction. A Will makes this process easier, less stressful, and less expensive for your loved ones after you're gone.

As a business owner, you need to think carefully about how your business is owned and what your intentions are for future ownership after your death or retirement. This is especially critical if you intend for family members to work for or share ownership of your business. Adult children make *a lot* of assumptions about their parents' property and "who gets what" after they die. Without being clear about your intentions from the beginning, you could unintentionally create serious issues for your loved ones after you pass away.

While we all hope we live long and healthy lives, no one knows when their last day on this Earth will be. If you don't have a Will and Powers of Attorney currently in place, do so now. These documents are easy to change in the future if needed. Many people will change their Will several times throughout their lives, and that's perfectly fine. Work with a competent local attorney to ensure the documents are drafted correctly to ensure acceptance and prevent anyone from challenging the documents.

Your company's legal documents also need to be very clear, not only about who has the authority to act for the company but also about what happens to the ownership of the company when an owner passes away. Therefore, I highly recommend reading Chapter 7 in this book (*Reduce Your Tax Burden*) to ensure your business has the right documents in place as well. Now is the time to protect your empire. You *are* your business. Do not overlook your personal, legal, and financial health!

Karen Hulme Alegi is an attorney in Maryland. She was in private practice for 20 years, representing clients in litigation and transactional matters. A significant part of Karen's practice included domestic relations matters, guardianship proceedings, and estate planning. Karen ultimately focused her firm's practice on Wills and Powers of Attorney so her clients would be prepared for all of life's challenges. Throughout her career, she has strived to educate and inform others about the easy steps everyone can take to protect themselves and their loved ones in declining health, either as a caregiver or one who needs care.

Karen continues to manage her real estate empire and works for the Office of Attorney General of Maryland. She resides in Gaithersburg with her family and (too many) pets. She is active in her local community and enjoys volunteering her time at animal shelters and with organizations that give people second chances. In her free time, you can find her in secondhand stores and antique markets looking for the next treasure!

Connect with Karen:

Instagram: https://www.instagram.com/karenalegiattorney/

LinkedIn: https://www.linkedin.com/in/karen-hulme-alegi/

Chapter 23

Smart Retirement Planning for Business Owners

The Secrets to Securing Your Future

Janine Jennings

Dedicated to Rodney, Janine Jr, Janine II, Eugene, Alfreda, and Linda

You can't save your way to riches without a strategy

My Story

What I survived would kill most people.

What comes to your mind when you say the word *Christmas*? The love, joy, and peace you have, right? My first daughter, my second child, was born on Christmas day, so you can imagine the joy she brought. At three months old, she wasn't feeling well, and I took her to the doctor all week. As a mother, my gut knew something was wrong regardless of what the pediatrician said. Saturday after work from the salon, I went to the

ER because she wasn't getting better. The ER turned into the ICU after five minutes, and I was told, "She won't live another day without a heart transplant."

She had severe dilated cardiomyopathy. My heart dropped. I was confused. I took her to the pediatrician all week, and they never said anything was wrong. After three weeks, the heart surgeon put her at the top of the transplant list for a heart.

She spent three months in the ICU and three months in the comfort of our home, along with my three-year-old son and their father, while she was waiting for the transplant. A side note: their father wasn't emotionally, mentally, or financially present then. That meant that I had to work, take my son back and forth to school, keep the house in order, run errands, go to doctor's appointments, manage my daughter's 24-hour care nurses, and be at the hospital by 6 pm to relieve my mother, who watched my daughter during the day for me when she was in the ICU. I stayed all night until it was time to take my son to school and prepare for work.

Every night, while waiting for her heart, as I sat by my daughter's bedside, I couldn't shake the feeling that I was failing her. The guilt was all-consuming, and I questioned every choice I made. *Was I a bad mother for having to work? Shouldn't I be able to provide the financial security that allowed me to stay by her side at every moment?*

The shame of needing to rely on my mother was another layer of my burden. My son, at just three years old, was growing up too fast, understanding more about illness and stress than any child should. I felt like I was robbing him of his childhood, and that thought broke my heart.

At work, the fear that I wasn't doing enough haunted me. Each task, each client, felt like it was taking me further away from my daughter. The worry that she might need me and I wouldn't be there was paralyzing. But the reality was that the bills didn't stop, and I had to keep working to keep us afloat because nobody was coming to save me.

My daughter received a heart but didn't survive the transplant; the guilt and shame hit me like a tidal wave. I started to blame myself for being unable to be there every second of the day and for not having saved enough money to make that possible. It was a dark period filled with self-blame and sorrow.

But in that darkness, I found a new resolve. I vowed to be better prepared for any future challenges. After my daughter's funeral, while grieving, we conceived another daughter; I was super happy. I relentlessly rebuilt the clientele I lost due to my non-flexible schedule. I started planning, saving, and making financial decisions that would allow me to be there for my family for whatever curveball life threw my way. By being disciplined in my saving techniques, I could afford to attend tax and business conferences to learn strategies to help me give top-tier service to my hair and tax clients. In this busy time of rebuilding my businesses, raising two children, paying for personal development courses, going through a divorce, and being a single parent, I graduated from John Carroll University in the top 5% of my class with Business, Accounting, Entrepreneurship, and Psychology degrees. This experience taught me the importance of preparation and resilience. The guilt and shame still linger, but now, sheer determination drives me to honor my daughter's memory by being the best mother I can be. I'm committed to helping four billion business owners save money on their taxes, get their books in order, organize their spending, become Quintillionaires, and retire with awareness.

My name is Janine Jennings. I'm the President of JP Tax Service and Accounting and the President of Cultural Differences Salon. For the past 30 years, I've educated myself on wealth creation and management, accounting, business tax saving strategies, and retirement planning. I help business owners secure their future by guiding them with the secrets of money-saving tax strategies, building generational wealth, and retirement planning.

The Strategy

Welcome to the J.P. Taxers community!

My name is Janine, and I represent J.P. Tax Service and Accounting. If you're a business owner aged 27-59+ and haven't started saving for retirement, don't worry. I've created a straightforward and practical guide to help you. It covers a step-by-step plan to get you on track to a $500,000+ retirement fund, even if you're starting from scratch. The S.T.A.R. method (Set Up financial goals, Track your expenses for Tax preparedness, Age with Awareness, Retire with Awareness) is designed to empower you with a concrete approach to managing your money.

In this guide, we are focusing on the "R" - Retire with Awareness.

I've been in the tax business for over 24 years, helping individuals secure their future. It's never too late to start saving. Many of my clients began with less than $1000, and with our guidance, they were able to build up $30,000 to $50,000 in just a few years. Their success stories can inspire you.

This retirement guide is not a one-size-fits-all solution. It's a flexible, customizable approach based on years of experience. It's designed to be simple and actionable, serving as a stepping stone to your retirement journey. If you need assistance, J.P. Tax Service and Accounting is here to help. Schedule a one-on-one coaching session to start your personalized retirement plan as soon as possible!

https://calendly.com/jptaxservicewealth/wealth-creation-call

Legal Disclaimer:

This retirement guide is for informational purposes only and doesn't serve as legal, financial, or investment advice. J.P. Tax Service, its owners, employees, and affiliates are not licensed financial advisors or legal professionals. The content in this guide is based on general information available at the time of publication and may change without notice.

No Guarantees:

While we strive to provide accurate and current information, the strategies, tips, and suggestions presented in this guide may not be suitable for all individuals or situations. Financial circumstances vary significantly among individuals.

Step 1: Know Your Starting Point

First, figure out your current financial situation to get a clear picture.

Calculate Your Net Worth: Add your assets (cash, property, investments) and subtract your debts. The result is your net worth.

Assets (What You Own)

- Cash: Include checking and savings account balances.
- Investments: Stocks, bonds, mutual funds, retirement accounts (401(k), I.R.A.).
- Property: Real Estate, vehicles, collectibles, and other personal property.
- Business Assets: The value of your business, equipment, inventory, and accounts receivable.
- Total Assets = Cash + Investments + Property + Business Assets
- Liabilities (What You Owe)
- Mortgages: Any remaining balance on your home or business property.
- Loans: Personal loans, business loans, car loans, student loans.
- Credit Card Debt: Total outstanding balance.
- Other Debts: Any other debts you owe.

Total Liabilities = Mortgages + Loans + Credit Card Debt + Other Debts

Where do you stand? Total Assets - Total Liabilities = Net Worth

Use the Excel workbook provided by J.P. Tax Service and Accounting to calculate your net worth easily: https://www.jptaxservice.com/tax-resources

*Clear out all numbers before putting in your own.

Evaluate Your Business: Your business is a big part of your wealth. Know its value and potential.

- Valuation: Get your business professionally valued to understand its worth.

Evaluate Your Social Security: Create an account at SSA.gov to know and understand the amount of money you will receive when you retire. You need 40 credits to receive social security payments.

Staying on top of your social security information is essential to your financial health and retirement planning.

Step 2: Set Clear Goals

Think about your financial goals for retirement. Set targets that are realistic yet ambitious.

Choose Your Retirement Age: Consider what retirement age suits your lifestyle. Starting to save earlier will give your money more time to grow.

If you want to retire earlier, use this survival number calculator to calculate how much money you will need to live off at retirement.

You can find the Survival Number Calculator here:

https://www.jptaxservice.com/tax-resources

When choosing a retirement age, ask yourself these questions:

- What do you want to do in retirement?
- Where and how do you want to live?
- Do you want to pay for a house, car, boat, etc.?
- Will you be taking care of parents, children, or grandchildren?

Starting at age 52, determine where your main and vacation homes will be, preferably in a state with no state taxes.

Tip: Consider having a walk-in tub for a ranch-style retirement house.

A reasonable housing budget should range between $500 and $700 per month in retirement.

Estimate Your Needs: Aim for a rough annual estimate of $50,000 to $60,000 in today's dollars.

Set a Savings Target: Aim to save $500,000 initially. It's a solid foundation.

Money is freedom—a freedom to be, do, and have a life you want to live and have dreamed of living. - Janine

Step 3: Start Saving Now

This is where the magic happens. Get those savings rolling. A Roth IRA is a great way to save for retirement because your contributions grow tax-free, and withdrawals in retirement are also tax-free.

Open a Retirement Account: Consider a Roth IRA, SEP IRA, or Solo 401(k). They all have their perks. (Suggested platforms: Acorns, Griffin, and Vanguard - free to set up)

You can find Acorns at http://bit.ly/4c4Erag.

Consider investing $120 to $150 a week toward your goal.

Understanding Your Investment Options:

1. Roth IRA: This retirement account allows your investments to grow tax-free. You contribute after-tax dollars, and qualified withdrawals in retirement are tax-free.
2. Self-Directed IRA: This offers more investment choices than a traditional IRA. You can invest in real estate, private companies, and more. It provides greater flexibility but requires more knowledge and oversight.
3. SEP IRA: This is designed for self-employed individuals and small business owners. Contributions are tax-deductible, and you can contribute a significant portion of your income, making it a powerful tool for high earners.
4. Annuity: This is an insurance product that provides a steady income stream, typically for life, in return for a lump sum or periodic payments.
5. Over-Funded Indexed Universal Life Insurance (IUL): This type of permanent life insurance includes a death benefit and a cash value component, which can grow based on an equity index.
6. Solo 401(k): This is for self-employed individuals or small business owners with no employees. It offers high contribution limits and tax advantages, allowing for substantial retirement savings.

Roth IRA Eligibility: Ensure you meet the income requirements to contribute to a Roth IRA. For 2024, you can contribute the full amount if your modified adjusted gross income (MAGI) is less than $153,000 (single) or $228,000 (married filing jointly).

Roth IRA Contribution Limits: For 2024, you can contribute up to $6,500 per year or $7,500 if you're over 50.

Roth Monthly Contributions: To maximize your contributions, aim to save $541.67 per month ($6,500 per year).

Increase Contributions Annually: As your business grows, your savings should too.

Retirement Planning Milestones

The Strategy	Age 50 -make catchup contributions up to $1000 dollars more annually -create digital products/and online courses	Age 55 -if you aren't working, you possibly can access a 401(k) plan without penalties	Age 59.5 -yay! You may qualify to take withdrawals from 401(k)/ IRAs without penalties
Retirement	Age 62 You can start to claim Social Security -benefits will increase 8% each year you delay	Age 65 Medicare Day! You can sign up for medicare. What will health insurance look like for you?	Age 66/67 Full retirement age (as considered in the eyes of Social Security) you DON'T have to retire at this time, its your choice
Retirement Distributions	Age 70 Last call for Social Security! Now is the time to start taking the benefits. FYI, Social Security maxes out at 132% of the initial full benefit	Age 73 Happy birthday! You have until April 1st to take the 1st required minimum distribution (RMD) from your IRA/or employer sponsored retirement plans and until next December to take the 2nd distribution	Age 75 Invest in an Immediate Annuity (250k) offer payments for life, mitigating the risk of outliving your assets.

Step 4: Invest Wisely

Saving is just the beginning. Now, it's time to make your money work for you. Here are some tips to help you invest wisely:

1. Diversify: Spread your investments across different assets, such as stocks, bonds, and real estate, to keep your portfolio balanced.

2. Stocks: Consider investing in the S&P 500, which has historically provided strong returns over the long term.

Note: You cannot directly trade the S&P 500 index itself. Instead, you can trade various financial products that track its performance, such as SPDR S&P 500 Trust (S.P.Y.), iShares Core S&P 500 (I.V.V.), and Vanguard S&P 500 (V.O.O.).

3. Dividend Kings: Consider investing in companies that have a history of increasing dividends for over 50 years. Some top dividend kings are:

- Coca Cola with a yield of 2.99%
- Altria with a yield of 8.39%
- Target with a yield of 2.70%
- 3M with a yield of 4.85%
- Starbucks with a yield of 2.87%

Money Nugget:

Consider creating digital products, such as ebooks and courses. These products offer scalability and the potential to monetize your expertise.

4. Real Estate:

Invest in rental properties for consistent rental income and potential appreciation. You can also consider buying a four to five-suite apartment building with a Self Directed I.R.A., selling it, and depositing the proceeds into the I.R.A. to build your retirement savings quickly.

5. U.S. Treasury Bonds:

Consider investing in 10-Year Treasury Notes for safety, liquidity, and tax advantages. You can purchase them through the U.S. Department of the Treasury or any brokerage account.

Rebalance Annually:

Check and adjust your investment portfolio yearly to stay on track.

Get Advice:

Don't hesitate to consult a trusted financial advisor for investment advice.

For more information, visit https://calendly.com/jptaxservicewealth/wealth-creation-call.

Money Nugget:

Consider following these top six investors:

- Ray Dalio
- Jon and Pete Najarian
- Paul Tudor Jones
- Mellody Hobson

- Daymond John
- Arlan Hamilton

Step 5: Maximize Your Business Value

Your business can be your ticket to a great retirement. Here's what you can do to maximize its value:

1. Plan Succession:
   Whether you plan to sell or pass on your business, it's important to have a succession plan in place.

2. Boost Profitability:
   Look for ways to increase your business's bottom line to maximize its value.

3. Valuation:
   Get your business professionally valued to understand its worth.

4. Invest Proceeds:
   If you sell your business, consider investing the proceeds into your retirement accounts.

5. Keep Finances Separate:
   It's easier to manage and eventually sell your business if you keep its finances separate.

I hope this helps!

Remember the following information: Let JP Tax Service and Accounting assist you with planning a strategy that's best for you.

Step 6: Protect Your Assets

You've worked hard for this. Protect it.

Insurance: Health, life, and disability insurance are essential. JP Tax Service and Accounting can provide a list of insurance companies that best fit your situation.

Create an Estate Plan: A will, power of attorney, and healthcare directive are essential. Get these in place. J.P. Tax Service and Accounting will assist you in creating these documents.

Consider a Trust: For larger estates, it offers protection and flexibility.

- Irrevocable trust: This offers benefits such as reduced estate taxes, asset protection from creditors, and controlled asset distribution. These terms cannot be altered after the assets are transferred. It's essential to consult with an experienced estate planning attorney to ensure it aligns with your specific needs and goals.
- Revocable trust: This is a versatile and powerful estate planning tool that provides flexibility, privacy, and control over your assets. It allows for seamless management in the event of incapacity and helps ensure that your estate is handled according to your wishes with minimal legal complications. Consulting with an estate planning attorney can help you tailor this trust to your specific needs and goals.

Step 7: Monitor and Adjust

Keep an eye on your progress and make adjustments as needed.

Track Your Progress: Use financial software such as: YNAB- EveryDollar- CreditKarma-Empower Personal Wealth. Check in regularly.

Adjust for Life Changes: Life happens. Be ready to tweak your plan.

- Bank accounts- have a Paid on Death (POD) Form attached to your non-business bank accounts, even if you are married
- Assets - have a Transfer on Death Form (TOD) in place; even if you are married

Stay Educated: The financial world changes. Keep learning.

*Money Wisdom: Numbers give you certainty—the more you measure, the more you manage.

Conclusion

Alright, let's do this! Don't let guilt or regret hold you back. Start today and build the future you deserve. With a solid plan and commitment, you can hit that $500,000+ mark and beyond.

Remember, it's a journey, not a race. Start small, stay committed, and keep your eyes on the horizon. You've built a successful business; now it's time to build a successful retirement.

Need a co-pilot? J.P. Tax Service and Accounting is here to help. Together, we'll make sure your retirement is as legendary as a Harley on the open road. Call us today to schedule your one-on-one retirement strategy session!

Let's ride into the future. You've got this.

Talk soon,

Janine

JP Tax Service and Accounting

P.S.S.

Get Your Organized Financial Awareness Checklist today!

https://jptaxx.activehosted.com/f/1

For many of you, this may feel overwhelming. Or perhaps you simply want additional support. This is why I created my Organized Financial Awareness checklist.

This free gift will break down additional information in a simple checklist, allowing you to break it down into small, bite-size chunks. My goal is for you to walk away confident and clear on what next step you need to take today.

Don't worry, I've got you. Sign up for the Organized Financial Awareness checklist today, and you will have your:

- Roadmap to financial success.
- Clarity on what step you need to take next.
- A simple document to refer back to easily.
- Stop second-guessing or lying awake at night stressed about money.

I never want you to feel like you have to do it alone. I don't want you to feel like you have to place your financial wellness in the hands of someone you ultimately can't really trust.

You deserve a life of financial freedom.

You deserve a life without fear of what life will throw your way.

You deserve a life full of confidence in your financial decisions.

Janine Jennings is the President of JP Tax Service and Accounting, a 5-Star Google-reviewed trusted accounting firm specializing in tax advisory services, business tax saving strategies, retirement planning, wealth creation and management, and accounting. She has 30 years of expertise in the cosmetology field, 24 years in the tax and accounting field, and her company has helped thousands of business owners save money on their taxes, calculate their profit margins, organize spending, and secure their future with a kick-ass retirement strategy. JP Tax Service and Accounting is making history with their S.T.A.R method and knowing your «Quintillionaire» number, one business owner at a time.

The community is over 400+ business owners, and the mission is to organize spending to increase more money to buy income-producing assets. Join us on Facebook in the JP Tax Service and Accounting group, where we talk money, mindset, and tax-saving loopholes, and hacks. Have a question about your taxes or money? Book a wealth creation call with our money team!

Janine is a mother of three beautiful children (two living), (freshly high school graduated), a cat grandma, an author, a speaker, a tax coach, and a Quintillionaire who is convinced that taxes are numbers that lead to bigger numbers for a better outcome. She is passionate about helping people figure out what is best for them and to save money on their taxes while doing so.

Connect with Janine:

Instagram: instagram.com/jenningspeytontaxservice
Website: https://www.jptaxservice.com/
Facebook: facebook.com/JPTaxServices

Twitter: twitter.com/JpTaxService

TikTok: tiktok.com/@jptaxservice

Books for tax saving strategies and retirement planning:
https://www.amazon.com/shop/janinej9stein

Email: janine@jptaxservice.com

Chapter 24

Discernment

Your Ninja Move for Next-Level Business Decisions
Laura Di Franco, MPT, Publisher

> *If I had to start over, I'd trust my gut instincts sooner to ensure decisions that aligned with love, joy, and gratitude. I'd bet on myself first.*

My Story

"It's nothing personal. It's just business."

Really?

Have you ever delayed firing someone, knowing in your gut that they were the wrong person for the job, but dreading the decision because you're nice, you like the person, and you're afraid of them hating you afterward?

"Hire slowly, fire quickly"—I didn't learn this lesson fast enough.

My ninja-level moves of awareness and discernment seemed to shut down when I had to do hard things like let someone go. Especially someone I knew was doing their best.

Welcome to building your perfect team and actually growing your business.

This isn't working. I've given him so many chances to prove himself. This doesn't feel right. But I've put so much time into this! So much money spent. Ugh! Maybe I'll give it one more month.

I talked myself into "one more month" or "one more week," so many times I cringe to think of the lost revenue I created by procrastinating.

Like my marriage, I waited for a dealbreaker rather than trusting my intuition months earlier and taking action the first time. It was easier to be confused because that meant I didn't have to make the hard decision or take the action I dreaded. The feeling inside was obvious—heavy, constricting, bad. In fact, it was consistently so far from the "Hell yes!" of alignment for me that I worried.

What is happening? Why am I falling asleep like this again? I know better!

What about when you become friends with a client?

Watch out, world, she's actually making a friend out of her perfect ideal client. She must be insane, and she's definitely doing it all wrong.

It takes courage to do business differently, doesn't it? My business *is* personal. My clients are friends. I actually care about them beyond the transaction. And I don't separate business and life. My business is my purpose and legacy—it *is* my life. I happen to do it while prioritizing the people (family, partner, and friends) I love.

Wow, can we do that?

Yes, you can do that. You must have the awareness and discernment that gives you a next-level path to what's in alignment with you. Think joy, love, and gratitude here. Feeling these is your superpower.

By the way, you'll never feel the clarity, courage, or confidence first. Take the action, and then you'll enjoy those feelings. This takes cojones, y'all. Big ones. And alignment. When you can discern between what's aligned and what's not, you become a ninja in life and business. I feel a little like a ninja now.

I didn't say the process is easy. Some days, I have the discernment and still can't take action on the decision I know I need to make. I don't want to crush people, but this *is* business. But now, there's much less time between the awareness of the alignment and the decision because I know how much harder it is to wait with the worry than actually jump and take action. I've trained well and built the action-taking muscles. You should see my action-biceps!

Taking action with fear and uncertainty is scary. It takes a warrior to leap with the faith that the wings will appear. But when you know for sure (you can feel the difference in your body), it's so much easier. It's not a guessing game anymore. You don't have to experiment when you trust what you feel and can act on that clarity.

This requires noticing and stepping into more of the **brave spaces** in your life. These spaces are opportunities. It pays to recognize where to look and what to do when you find them.

Here is my poetic version of that how-to.

Brave Spaces
By Laura Di Franco

I feel brave spaces
between the hush of my breath
and the midnight stars
stuck in that sweet knot in my throat
as inspiration shifts it a bit
and it slides from my heart to my tongue
and begins to sound like a song
written about your smile.

Dark hours hold some
before dawn
before the first bird song
before I commit
to fully living that day.
I pray for more light:
"Please, illuminate my why
no matter what the naysayers say."

I catch one like a firefly
carefully cupping it to my face
peeking at the glow
hoping for a trace of magic
something to show me
I'm meant for this world
that I belong
that my voice matters
that you see my heart.

I start finding parts in the pain
in the center of the rocks
harder as the clock ticks
knowing about the treasure
like geodes
If, oh gee, only I'm brave enough
patient enough
strong enough
to dig deeper

wake from the sleep
notice the weight of five decades of shoulds
piled on my soul plate.
Brave spaces rest in those layers
where curiosity is gold
and I'm sold on peeling them away one by one
until I'm free
can breathe
feel like me again.

Nowadays, all I need to do
is gaze at the sunrise sky
notice the still points in my life
between slower in and exhales
the choice between fear and love
the pause of my pen
before the next line
the rhyme in line nine.

I realize brave spaces
are everywhere we stop
drop into the present of the moment
get under the fire of our mind
to find "Will they like me?"
and spin a different tune to the mirror.
"Hey, love warrior, I see you. Come and play!
Saving the world works better
when you love yourself first today."

Where are the brave spaces in your life?
Hiding in plain sight.
Cowering in old stories of blame
energy lodged in your gut
a web of shame setting the table to feed
off the chaos, mess, and uncertainty
banking on your inability

to just be and feel.
And there it is again my friends,

Brave Healers. . .
. . .you know how to feel.
You've connected to the most mind-blowing
magic in all the land
Put your hand on your heart
sink in for a while
let the Divine soul that is you
take the wheel.

Open her up
on a road you haven't traveled
as much.
Feel the wind in the stillness.
the excitement and purpose in your fear.
Instead of riding the brake
using anxiety as the fuel in your tank
trust and squeeze the gas pedal
get a little Thelma and Louise on life's ass.

It's always good to remind yourself
at the end of this ride
the goal isn't getting out alive.
Dive into every brave space in your life
your heart, your mind, and your alien soul
like never before
Dance, sing, play, paint, and write
through the pain
and especially the joy.

Brave is so much better
when joy shouts, "Shotgun!"
and the two as one, take the darkness on
Each space, each step,
each curve of your words lights the path.
Keep going until breathing syncs up
the lines of truth start to blur
and the sound between your sigh and the stars
is, "I love you."

When it's time to take your next step, and you feel the angst in your gut, hear that inner critic buzzing its crap in your ear, and feel like going back to bed, pause and breathe. Use your "phone a friend" option. Don't sit in it by yourself. Don't allow another moment of negative, unhelpful, unhealthy thoughts to bring your sexy, badass, hippie, warrior-love self down.

You matter, and so does your vision for your business. It's time to love having enough energy, money, freedom, time, and resources to generously take care of yourself and everyone you love and serve. You don't get there by wallowing in fear or worry thoughts. You get there by going ninja on fear's ass and doing something your future self will thank you for.

Refine your vision and purpose, and place those details in front of you every single day. Remind yourself often. Get the hot pink sticky notes and neon highlighters out. Put up the gigantic whiteboard and your favorite quote art. Craft a manifesto for your life and frame it in gold glitter sparkle.

When making decisions, use discernment (the ultimate ninja move of awareness) and feel if it's aligned with your vision. You will feel it! It's clear. Remember, confusion is not a "Hell yes!" Don't say yes to stuff your body is saying no to, no matter what anyone says, or how shiny the object is.

The discernment for the "Hell yes!" is the feeling of joy. What does pure joy feel like in your body? This is a unique feeling only you get to describe. Nobody else gets to try to help you with this, no matter how wise or experienced they are. Get good at knowing the answer to how joy feels. And let every choice be something that fills you with that rocket fuel.

One of my business friends practices discernment by talking about his 2+ people and experiences. If it's not a 2+ conversation, he isn't having it. These are the conversations, people, situations, and collaborations that leave you feeling like a better person, fired up with inspiration, and uplifted—aligned with life and your purpose.

As entrepreneurs, we can't afford anything less than a 2+ experience, and when we settle, we burn out. I want you to get so good at this practice that you never experience burnout or worse—pain, illness, or disease. That's what happens when you constantly compromise your soul's purpose, voice, and dreams, ignore what brings you joy, and fall prey to the duties and obligations you've been taught should bring you success and happiness.

Here's a tool to help you practice this kind of awareness in your life and business, the kind where you never have regrets about the risks you take, the investments you make, or the brave actions you practice on your journey.

The Strategy

Bodyfulness: Decisions Made Easy

Grab a piece of notebook paper and draw a line down the middle in the center, making two columns, right and left.

At the top of the left column, write the heading "Hell yes!" and at the top of the right column, write the heading "Hell no."

Begin by asking yourself: *What does a "Hell yes!" event feel like in my body?* Think about describing that feeling. What are the sensations?

My "Hell yes!" moments feel warm and strong. There's an upright posture and a smile on my face.

Begin to list all the ways you feel when you're experiencing these moments in your left-hand column. Example:

Warm
Strong
Flexible
Smiling

Now do the same for the "Hell no!" This is when something's not feeling good or right. Your body is saying *no*. When I feel a "Hell no!"

it feels tight; there's a knot in my throat, and I feel cold. Make your list on the right side of all the ways you know something is a no for you. Describe all the ways you sense or notice that. If you've written a word like *sad* or *bad*, try to describe where and how that feels in your body. Example:

Tight
Constricting
Cold
Pouting

The trick here is to create a cheat sheet for yourself so you can learn your body's GPS system, the language it speaks every single day when it's trying to help you make decisions for your life and business that align with your soul and purpose.

Many people also rely on their clair-senses of feeling, knowing, or hearing. You other-level psychically connected badasses have a strong connection, but I often hear you doubting decisions due to fear.

You need a cheat sheet, too!

Many ask me, "What happens when you're trying to decide and the answer is 'I don't know' or 'I'm confused'?"

The answer: An 'I don't know' (or confusion or grey area) is not a "Hell yes!" so it's a no.

This has given me so much clarity. I just have to listen. It's always clear. It's a matter of whether or not I'm willing to listen and follow those signs rather than talk myself into something different or make excuses for why I'm saying yes when my body is clearly saying no. We're good at that, aren't we? I know I've been a master at that!

When my business increased from five to multi-six figures in a short amount of time, I asked myself: *Are you really willing to sabotage your mind, body, and soul for success because you think it's something you need to do rather than actually listening to your soul tell you it is or isn't?*

Dude. The answer is no. I listen now. And you can, too.

You're not doing business as usual, and we know it!

We got you. You *can* do business on your own terms. You can do this! Let's talk about community next (and last) because it's part of the answer to how we do this.

Read more about Laura in the About the Author section below.

BraveHealer.com

Chapter 25

Success Isn't a Solo Gig
A Community-Building Strategy for Next-Level Growth
Laura Di Franco, MPT, Publisher

> *The first thing you need to realize about your business is that other people make it a success. Building and leading a community that wants to help you build your big-ass vision is how you create an empire.*

My Story

When one person shows up to your Zoom (when you wanted 30), take a breath. *That* one person is your "community," and it's enough to start.

Everyone starts at zero. I did. As a physical therapist, I had 150 people on my email list, but when I started blogging and Facebooking, it increased to several hundred. It's in the tens of thousands now, with a community of thousands of authors who believe in me and my vision and are helping me build it. It took me eight years to get there, building a community of like-minded badasses to play with.

Community is everything and *together* is how you do this.

For one of my first Zoom workshops, I remember the one person who showed up live. Ilana. Thank you, Ilana. She was a naturopathic doctor who felt confused about her ideal client and about the lack of alignment she felt about her offerings. "I'm tired of guessing," she said.

Me too, Ilana, me too.

"Well, I guess it's just the two of us today. Thank you for being here. Let's see if I can help you with your business!"

At that point, I adopted an attitude that went something like: "If one person shows up, then pour everything you can into that one person. Then schedule another workshop and do it again."

I remember getting that business advice from a coach named Torrie. "You're not just scheduling one workshop date. Make sure you're scheduling the next one, too."

I created my Facebook group, Brave Badass Healers, A Community for World-Changers, to serve current and prospective ideal clients and build community. I started by creating inspiring content and quickly realized a community-building strategy required more effort than some cute "show me your pets" posts. Although I do love a furry friends share.

When I dabbled with free workshops and webinars, things changed for me. They were easy to repeat, and I got to know people who had questions I could answer. I love teaching, so teaching workshops totally lit me up.

Don't ask what the world needs. Ask what makes you come alive, and go do it. Because what the world needs is people who have come alive.
~Howard Thurman

Oh, Howard, you got it, man. This is it! What makes you come alive? Go do more of it.

Teaching and coaching are my passions. I absolutely get excited, sit up taller, talk louder, and get a little alien-crazy when I teach or coach people on how to write, tell their stories, and build their communities and businesses. I learned my own language of coming alive.

What's yours? You'll feel it in your body!

I came alive with Ilana that day. She had a huge aha by the end of the hour (essentially a one-on-one business coaching session).

"OMG, I said yes to this, but actually, it's been bothering me ever since. This isn't aligned at all!"

I changed her life and business that day, and she wrote me a very cool testimonial about it.

That was the beginning of sharing more wisdom and doing more teaching through a community-building workshop or event that wasn't just meant to create income but to allow people to get to know me at the next level and build relationships. I admittedly now have trouble remembering all the badass healers in my community because there are so many. It's a good problem to have. This problem helped me get some huge clarity about the vision of my business and what exactly I wanted for my future.

I realized *scaling* wasn't in my near future, but *growth* was.

Everyone thinks scaling their business is what they want because every business coach on the planet sells the "7-Figure Blueprint." If I see this one more time, I may choke. Shit, I fell for it! Maybe some of you remember the "7-Figure Healer" title I used for my networking event for about a week?

Picture the clouds parting and God herself showing her face through the stars to say, "Laura, here's the answer to everything." That is how I felt about this aha.

I want something different. I want an inheritable business that allows my legacy to continue through brave souls who were born to do this with me. Books are a legacy business. I've already achieved this success. I'm already there. I'm already basking, y'all.

I want to grow (lifelong learner here). Go read Chapter 20 for backup on that topic.

I don't need to find more people like me to do the things only I can do (even though I do know those people exist). I want to build something that stays intimate, healing, and personal, creates deeper connections, and ripples out from me through my clients and partners.

I don't have to scale this to something I can't manage or have to hire another CEO, COO, or other C-Crap titled person for. I don't have to do this "business as usual." I can want what I want and create something that helps me thrive and generously take care of myself and everyone I love.

When you're out in the big, bad world of the internet and every single message is marketing that 7-figure and beyond kind of thing, you start to think you want it, without even doing any numbers! Do the numbers! Read Chapters 8 and 23 and let my friends Holly and Janine help you with those numbers! Don't get paralyzed by this. The numbers are freedom. Shoot, I'm even banging the computer keys harder as I try to push my excitement into this page for you.

It's this badass community of brave healers who created this with me. It's by being in and serving the community that I've succeeded and will continue to succeed beyond the current wild dreams I have. It's remembering that the one person on your Zoom who you're staring at **is your community**. It's remembering that the power lies in that precious moment. Everything is attraction. Who are you being in that moment? A worried pile of stress? A disappointed bag of what-if doubts?

Notice the thoughts: *Nobody's showing up. This sucks. I'm a failure. This isn't working.*

Change them: *One person showed up! Awesome! I'm gonna do my thing and then do it again!*

Continue to manifest some badassery with how you show up and be for that one person. Don't allow the stuff you're making things mean to dictate your energy and intention.

With awareness, you have a choice. And *that* is the ninja move.

You're building your community every day in every single interaction (every word, written or spoken).

And you're never alone. So, let's get started building this community!

The Strategy

Using a Group to Grow Your Community and Business

If you don't have a community group for your business yet, you'll need to think about your business goals, your branding (read Chapter 4), and the title of the group.

I run my group(s) on Facebook and using Zoom. Some business partners I know have migrated off of Facebook to other platforms. Facebook is free. Other platforms aren't. Do your research, figure out your bigger goals, and choose wisely.

3 Simple Steps to Creating a Community and Business-Building Group

1. Create a title that brands/markets your business, is clear, and is takeaway-oriented
2. Create and commit to a content strategy—take action
3. Be consistent, and don't give up

1. Title your group

Brave Badass Healers, A Community for World-Changers is quite a title, I know. I like it, people resonate with it, and it stuck. If I changed it today, I may do something boring like: The Brave Healer Business Growth Community. The first title is now ingrained into so much of my business offerings that I'd be dumb to try to change it. So, if you get to start from scratch, lucky you! Do it right the first time!

Be clear, not clever. Your group name will either attract perfect clients or not. I love the story my blogger mentor, Jon Morrow, founder of SmartBlogger, tells about how he devotes two of the ten hours he spends writing an article on the title alone. Titles are marketing. Hit me up for some title brainstorming—I'm such a geek when it comes to this. It's one of the places I come alive.

Think takeaway or results. What do your ideal clients want? You'll give them what they need in your programs, but what is their deepest desire? It's knowing what they want and then creating clear titles that express it that'll amplify everything you create. If you'd like some help getting clear about your ideal client and their deepest desires, please grab access to The Brave Healer Resources Vault and my Ideal Client Master Class: https://lauradifranco.com/resources-vault/

2. Content that builds community

You'll want to ask yourself: How do I want to serve in this group?

I want to provide coaching about writing, business-building, and publishing and to help you feel excited about sharing brave stories you haven't shared yet. I want to help you use writing as a healing tool and also to build your business. I want to inspire the shit out of you—move you into action even though you're feeling that purpose-driven fear. I want to help you master your mindset to ninja level.

All of these topics make me come alive. And I want to feel that feeling of being fiercely alive every day, especially when I'm serving people for free. If I feel burnout, it's a quick no (did you do the exercise in the last chapter?). Creating regular content that helps people engage is one great goal, but it also needs to make me come alive and be aligned with that joy.

This content can include written posts that ask engaging questions that people want to answer.

When I see the common question, "What's the biggest problem you're facing in your business?" on social media, you know what I do? Gag. It feels so inauthentic to ask a group a question for your own selfish purposes with the intent to sell them something. Some call this due diligence. I call it bullshit.

Save that due diligence for your ideal client homework. I'm not saying it's not a smart question to ask; I'm saying that in your community-building group, it's the wrong tactic.

There's a better way. Here are five community-building content ideas:

1. Ask questions that help people get to know themselves better.
2. Ask questions that take a little courage to answer.
3. Ask questions that help people share *their* wisdom with your group.
4. Ask questions to help others shine their light, wisdom, passion, purpose, and business.
5. Give **value** with your own wisdom, knowledge, solutions, and skills for free.

These are only a few of the ways you can engage your community. By the way, your content might be written, video, audio, or other. No rules. What does your ideal client consume more of? If you don't know, ask!

Giving others the stage is one of the most effective ways to lift others up that I've ever used. It's good vibes, y'all. It's uplifting, helpful, and brings the best out in people. When you help someone be their best, feel like a better, smarter person, or more aligned with their dreams, you win. Work on that.

The Community-Building Event

Events (workshops, webinars, open mics) are my favorite way to build community and grow my business. What workshop-style event could you run regularly that showcases your knowledge and helps give others the stage?

The Monday Morning Breakthroughs event is an example in my world. You'll find that housed in the free Facebook group (Brave Badass Healers, A Community for World-Changers) under the Events tab.

The event is on Zoom twice a month and is 75 minutes long. I've experimented with 60 and 90-minute sessions. I settled on the 75.

Lesson: Don't procrastinate on taking action until you think it's perfect or ready. Just hold an event, learn and grow, and do another one. Take action. It's how you'll create (and improve) the event.

There are many agendas that could work for your event. I love including the following pieces:

1. Teaching or coaching to provide practical value
2. Business development and networking to provide connection
3. Guest experts sharing their wisdom to provide a stage for A-list clients
4. A speaker's showcase to give others a stage
5. Giveaways and other fun stuff!

My goal for every event is to show up as my authentic self, not worry about what people think about me, and just be me and deliver value for those who show up. I set an intention to hold a safe space for expression, inclusion, and healing, and always practice grounding and centering in love and gratitude.

IMPORTANT:

The energy, intention, and authenticity matter more or as much as the content.

The vulnerable way you express yourself matters more or as much as the content.

The way you remember to give others a stage matters more than the content.

The way you express gratitude matters more or as much as the content.

Keys for success:

1. Create a regular, consistent time for your event and show up no matter how many RSVP.
2. Give it your all during the event, no matter how many people show up.
3. Ask for feedback and refine as you go.

Strategizing a business-building event with you is absolutely one of my favorite services. Hit me up for a strategy session. It's badass. You can email my team to set that up: support@LauraDiFranco.com

3. Consistency is Key to Success (Even When Things are Tough)

It doesn't matter if we're talking about your event, your email newsletter, your blog, or your workshops; consistency is more important than frequency. You're growing, building, and evolving along the way. Take consistent action and don't give up—that exact thing will be how you create and succeed.

A consistent action-taking strategy brought my business from the one-workshop level to an empire that serves thousands of healers.

And, not giving up is a success strategy.

You know that advice about not quitting because you're closer to success than you think? We can't see the big picture. We *can,* however, feel the momentum of our efforts and the "something big" coming. The problem is trusting it when you're having a bad day.

Don't quit. You can rest, but you're not allowed to give up. Clear your mind. Be a ninja.

Here are ten things you can do instead of giving up on your business dreams when you're having a rough day:

1. Reach out to someone and talk it out. Don't sit in it alone. This is so easy, yet many of us don't do it. Maybe shame or embarrassment keep you from wanting to talk about it. The thing is, we've all been there. Call someone.

2. Hire a business coach to help you get unstuck or light (or rekindle) your fire. Then, go read Chapter 21.

3. Journal out everything without censoring yourself. Try for at least 750 words and repeat this every day until something shifts. My tool in the book *How to Be Brave* will give you all the details.

4. Practice breathwork until you have an "experience." If you need a referral, reach out.

5. Put on some sound-healing music (or your favorite upbeat tune) and get into a zone where you can quiet your mind and shift the energy. ListeningtoSmile.com has some of my favorite sound healing and using the code BRAVE will get you a discount on albums.

6. Walk or exercise until you sweat a little, outside if possible. Nature will shift your energy, mood, and outlook.

7. Focus on one thing you love the most in your business and share (either journal it or talk to someone) about the what and why.

8. Go write a blog or social post to help your ideal client with a problem they're having. Helping others or defaulting to gratitude for serving others will help shift the energy. In fact, worry and fear can't exist at the same time as gratitude. Go for the gratitude in any small, medium, or large way. Journal it out.

9. Put your feet in the grass. Unless it's 30 below. Then go put your hands in some potted plants. Earthing is a powerful energy shifter.

10. Clean! The Feng Shui of cleaning and clearing your spaces is real magic. I've written entire chapters on this and how this one tool can create a shift so big that money shows up. For reals—checks in the mail, y'all. Start by cleaning and clearing the spaces you work and create in. Then, expand to all the rest of your living spaces. Hint: Your car is one of those.

Okay, you have the three simple steps to using a group to build your community and business. What's next? Doing it! I hope you're pen is moving on your notebook and you're strategizing how you'll serve in your new (or existing) group. Get into action today! Any small step matters!

And remember, you're not alone!

Read more about Laura in the About the Author section below. BraveHealer.com

Now What?

The experts here care about your success and they know how hard you work to bring your vision to life every day because they're doing it alongside you. If, before reading this book, you felt like your community was lacking, guess what? Look around; you have a badass community to play with now!

This is way more than a book. It's a generous community ready to answer your questions and provide support. Reach out, explore their sites, and get the support you want and need. Be brave!

Your biggest success will happen in community with the support of many. We're eager to be one of the communities you can count on to help you grow your business, succeed beyond your dreams, and leave your legacy in the world in a bigger way.

Come over and join Brave Badass Healers here: https://www.facebook.com/groups/YourHighVibeBusiness

And go back and re-read and practice some of the strategies from this book that resonated the most. Follow up with the authors! They're waiting to chat, give you some support, and answer a question!

Do you have a specific question for me, or do you want to do some networking? You can join one of our Brave Healer Power Hour private networking sessions by requesting the schedule link with a quick email: support@LauraDiFranco.com

Now, to end with the badassiest magical manifesting energy there is—gratitude!

A Rampage of Gratitude

To the stellar cast of co-authors who stepped up with their "Hell yes!" Thanks for walking beside me on this journey and for the love and support that keeps me burning in my purpose every day. Thank you for getting my collaborative spirit and for being here with yours.

To our Book Launch Team: You're such badasses. Thank you so much for coming back to read another one of our books and for the love and support you're pouring into this community. We love your Amazon reviews y'all. They keep us authors going on a bad day.

Melissa Henry: Thank you for working with me to create this brilliant cover art that spoke to my soul. You're talented beyond words. I'm in love with my Galaxy Girl.

Tanya Stokes: Thank you for the phenomenal cover design that helps bring this vision to life. You put your fierce and loving soul into everything you do, and it shows. It also creates magic for businesses.

Kelly vdH Kaschula (our interior designer and Brave Kids Books director): Thank you for helping us create a reader experience that shines. Each time you step up with your talent to help design one of our titles, I feel so much gratitude that you're a part of my team.

Maggie McLaughlin: Your Amazon and book expertise and care help our systems and processes run smoothly, and you bring a level of personal service to this that I'm so grateful for. Thank you for being a part of this vision and our team.

To my business coaches who've pushed and shoved, advised and suggested, counseled and coached this alien soul—thank you for tolerating my too-muchness in a way that helped me feel brave and that keeps me going on this journey every day.

To the people I love who put up with me and my "Brave Healer" visionary alien soul, thank you for loving me no matter what, believing in me, and helping me leave this legacy.

About the Author

Laura Di Franco, MPT, is the CEO of Brave Healer Productions, an award-winning publisher specializing in business strategy for healers and those who serve them. The publishing house includes Brave Kids Books and Brave Business Books and specializes in expert book collaborations. They offer programs that serve author-entrepreneurs well past their book launch.

Laura spent 30 years in holistic physical therapy (12 in private practice) before making the pivot to publishing. With 14 years of training in the martial arts, 13 of her own books, and a community of over 2000 authors (including over 80 Amazon bestsellers and counting), she knows how to help you share your brave words in a way that builds your business and your dream life.

Her daily mission is to help fellow holistic wellness professionals by paying forward everything she's learned in business and healing. She shares her authentic passion, wisdom, and expertise with refreshing transparency and straightforward badassery. Hold on to your seat because riding alongside her means you'll be pushed beyond your comfort zone and have way more fun with your purpose-driven fears on a regular basis.

When Laura chills out, you'll find her at a poetry event with friends, walking in the woods, driving her Mustang, bouncing to the beat at a rave, or on a beach in Mexico with something made of dark chocolate in her mouth. Joy is her compass and her business strategy.

Connect with Laura:

Websites:
https://BraveHealer.com

https://BraveKidsBooks.com

YouTube:
https://www.youtube.com/@bravehealerproductions2444

Facebook Business Page: https://www.Facebook.com/BraveHealerbyLaura/

Free Facebook Group:
https://www.facebook.com/groups/YourHighVibeBusiness

Instagram:
https://www.Instagram.com/BraveHealerProductions
https://www.instagram.com/bravekidsbooks/

LinkedIn: https://www.linkedin.com/in/laura-di-franco-mpt-1b037a5/

Good Morning Joy TV Episode:

https://youtu.be/vvYyMJGpP_U?si=Cbs5rTsbGRLsxfZS

BECOME A BESTSELLING AUTHOR

Your words change the world when you're brave enough to share them. It's time to be brave.

Are you ready to become an author in one of our bestselling books? Or lead your own book project? Brave Healer Productions, Brave Kids Books, and Brave Business Books are waiting for you!

Reach out to speak to the Brave Healer Productions publishing team by emailing: support@LauraDiFranco.com

The Brave Healer Transformation School

Ready to teach your business or health and wellness course online? We make that easy. Start earning passive income with your digital course!

https://bravehealertransformationschool.com/

The Brave Healer Writer's Circle

Want a safe space to write in a community and stay accountable to your goals? The Writer's Circle meets up to five times each month and provides the support, teaching, and accountability you're looking for. Check our schedule, including the guest writing experts coming to share their wisdom. Topics include business writing, writing to heal, creative fiction and non-fiction writing, and more!

https://lauradifranco.com/writers-circle/

If you want to take your business to empire level, at some point, you'll need to get over your purpose-driven fears, invest in yourself, your vision, and your business, and take the action your soul is yearning for you to take. You're not alone. Your message and work matter. You're worthy. That fear of not-good-enough is boring. This isn't about you anymore. It's about the life you'll save when you share your brave words. It's time to be brave.

With Warrior Love,

Laura
BraveHealer.com

Made in the USA
Middletown, DE
28 October 2024